POTLUCK PARADISE

POTLUCK
Paradise

Favorite Fare

FROM CHURCH & COMMUNITY COOKBOOKS

RAE KATHERINE EIGHMEY
and **DEBBIE MILLER**

Foreword by Dave Wood

MINNESOTA HISTORICAL SOCIETY PRESS

www.mhspress.org

The Minnesota Historical Society Press is a member of the Association of American University Presses.

Manufactured in the United States of America

10 9 8 7 6 5 4 3 2 1

♾ The paper used in this publication meets the minimum requirements of the American National Standard for Information Sciences—Permanence for Printed Library Materials, ANSI Z39.48–1984.

Cookbooks photo by Eric Mortenson, Minnesota Historical Society

Trademarked products:

Cool Whip® is a registered trademark of Kraft Foods

Jell-O® is a registered trademark of General Foods

Kitchen Bouquet® is a registered trademark of HV Food Products Company

Pepperidge Farm® is a registered trademark of Pepperidge Farm, Incorporated

Pyrex® is a registered trademark of Corning Incorporated

Tupperware® is a registered trademark of Tupperware Brands, Inc.

Ziploc® is a registered trademark of S. C. Johnson Brands

International Standard Book Number
ISBN 13: 978-0-87351-625-9 (paper)
ISBN 10: 0-87351-625-7 (paper)

Library of Congress Cataloging-in-Publication Data
Eighmey, Rae Katherine.
    Potluck paradise : favorite fare from church and community cookbooks / Rae Katherine Eighmey and Debbie Miller ; foreword by Dave Wood.
        p. cm.
Includes index.
    ISBN-13: 978-0-87351-625-9 (paper : alk. paper)
    ISBN-10: 0-87351-625-7 (paper : alk. paper)
    1. Cookery, American. I. Miller, Deborah L., 1948– II. Title.
TX715.E337 2008
641.5973—dc22

                                            2008008738

To those plucky midwestern homemakers of the 1950s, who
toted casseroles and hot dishes to countless church basements,
packed up pies for neighborhood gatherings,
baked millions of breads and cakes, raising billions of bake sale dollars,
filled cookie jars endlessly, feeding rampaging hoards of school children,
pulled pantry basics and refrigerator leftovers into delicious potluck suppers,
and wrote down all the recipes,
We dedicate this journey of rediscovery.

For Emma, Sally, and Nell, who went before, and for Liz and Chris, who follow. RKE

For Mom and Patty B. DM

 # CONTENTS

Rolled Molasses Cookies

Banana Spice Cookies

Minnesota Milk
ST. PAUL, MINNESOTA

W. A. LANG COMPANY
General Insurance · Life · Bonds

The Mixing Bowl

JUBILEE
Cook Book

WOMAN'S CLUB OF

CURRICULUM
for
COOKS

RECIPES
Out of The Blue

Official Photograph U. S. Air Force

Compiled by the

DULUTH
NON-COMMISSIONED
OFFICER'S WIVES CLUB
OF
DULUTH, MINNESOTA

President:
PAT MARTIN
Vice President:
VI KRUGER

Secretary:
MARY ANN SCRIBNER

Treasurer:
BROWN

U. S. AIR FORCE   FC-404

MOBILE RECIPES
lake church

Hilda's Date Cookies Drop

UNIVERSITY HOSPITAL
FACULTY WOMEN

FOREWORD

Dave Wood

VERY FEW BOOKS AND MAGAZINES graced our little house in Whitehall, Wisconsin, back in the 1940s and 1950s. The bookcase wasn't empty, of course, but held a multitude of my mother's African violets and old *Reader's Digests*. The books we did have were on one topic only: Food, food, and more food.

My mother was a very popular cook, restaurateur, and caterer in our little town. But she didn't own a Rombauer, or a Claiborne, or a Beard, or even the old General Mills loose-leaf. What she had was church cookbooks. She was way ahead of the ecumenical movement, for she had as many Catholic Church cookbooks as she had Lutheran. They were spiral-bound affairs, spattered with Crisco and lard and powdered sugar and Pillsbury's Best Flour.

I remember one day when she decided to make icebox cookies. She took the tattered books down from the cupboard, spread them out on the table, and turned to all the icebox cookie recipes. She consulted each recipe, chose the features she liked best in each one, and came up with an amalgamated icebox cookie roll to toss in the fridge for baking later. Authors Rae Eighmey and Debbie Miller have done much the same thing in the volume before you, so I'm pretty proud of my mother for being so avant-garde.

ALL GOOD THINGS MUST COME to an end, so after my mother died and my father had to move to the local nursing home, our family held an auction of household goods. I packed all the church cookbooks in one box, thinking to simplify the auctioneer's task. When auctioneer Eide saw what I had done, he said, "Are you nuts? I'm going to auction these separately, just like her souvenirs from Wisconsin Dells and Hayward."

So the auction began, and it went rather badly. My father, who was warned not to come from the nursing home, came anyway, and he turned purple when the year-old Coldspot upright freezer went for $15. After big bids on the souvenirs, Mr. Eide started on the cookbooks: Sts. Peter and Paul Catholic Church in Independence, the United Methodist in Whitehall,

Fagernes Church up on Brekke Ridge, and on and on. They all evoked spirited bidding and totaled more than what the newish dining room set brought. Finally came the pièce de résistance, the cookbook from our church, Our Saviour's Lutheran, published in 1948, a classic of the genre. My old man just shook his head when Trudy Bergum bid $18 for the flour-encrusted old tome. And that's the way it went.

READING THROUGH THESE PAGES of *Potluck Paradise*, with its recipes for Snickerdoodles and Cherry Nut Bread and Italian Spaghetti, I'm assaulted by good memories of my childhood and beyond, of Ladies' Aid afternoon luncheons every Tuesday at Our Saviour's, of family reunions beside muddy ponds in city parks all over Trempealeau County, Wisconsin. The long paper-covered picnic tables stick in my memory like burnt cheddar on the bottom of a depleted macaroni and cheese roaster.

Yes, bluestone roasters, crockery casseroles imprinted with a legend like "Buy at Bye's Store—Osseo, Wis." My mother's bright orange bowl always used for the salad made of tiny macaroni rings and canned miniature shrimp. The flat porcelain platters announcing the fiftieth anniversary of South Beaver Creek Lutheran Church, 1857–1907. What was in them, of course, was what counted. Like Mrs. Milton Strand's heavenly scalloped potatoes swimming in cream and butter and flecked with tiny tender Swedish meatballs. Or exotica like chow mein hot dish redolent of soy sauce and topped with fried noodles for crunch.

Then came Jell-O. Red stuff slathered with real whipped cream, Grandma Wood's lime Jell-O, which she made with 7-Up. (Don't tell anyone.) I avoided most of them because they reminded me of Technicolor lutefisk. Except for my Aunt Doris's special concoction: lemon Jell-O topped with mayonnaise and spiked with grated carrots and minced onion. ("Onion!" clucked the elderly president of the Rebekah Circle. "Those Johnsons are so *different!*")

Let's not forget the sandwiches, which rows of brawny-armed farmers in white starched dress shirts, sleeves rolled to mid forearms, piled on top of everything. Underwood potted ham smeared thinly on homemade bread. Glossy dried beef on buttered buns. Open-faced rullepolse sandwiches, if someone was really trying to show off (which you'd know when there was a strip of adhesive tape on the plate that said "Mrs. L. Overgaard").

I've learned more about nationality and sociology—and life—from church cookbooks than I ever did in school. I learned that German Lutherans ate more sauerkraut than their Norwegian compatriots across the synod. The Norwegians ate more sugar cookies. I learned that Polish Catholics actually simmered their bratwursts in beer that actually had alcohol in it. Uff da.

The bell choir at our church, Ascension Episcopal in Stillwater, recently published a cookbook which is heavy on *boeuf bourguignon* and asparagus recipes with recommendations for appropriate Cabernets and Malbecs accompanying each menu. (So who said Episcopalians were "the frozen chosen"?) Our Saviour's Lutheran was a tiny bit more Low Church. It leaned more toward miniature marshmallows in Glorified Rice. No reference was ever made to Mogen David, even though all good Lutherans drank that syrupy stuff while eating *fattigmand bakkels.* (There goes that ecumenicism again.)

Books like that and the cookbook before you also make for a slice of delicious history. I remember as a lad in the 1940s reading recipes in the Our Saviour's classic. I saw a very fancy recipe that called for stuffing a steak with select oysters, submitted by Mrs. Carl Olson, who lived in a grubby one-room apartment that smelled of kerosene in the back of the Texaco station, where I delivered Mr. Olson's *Winona Republican-Herald.* "Boy," I said, "I didn't think they could afford stuff like that!"

"They can't," replied my father. "Old Man Olson lost everything in the stock market crash in '29."

That's history—not sweet, but close to the bone.

PREFACE

Rae Katherine Eighmey and Debbie Miller

WHEN WE BEGAN TO WORK on *Potluck Paradise*, we looked at the many community cookbooks in the Minnesota Historical Society library's collection that had been published in the 1950s. We read through them together, side by side, at a library table, talking about what recipes we expected to find based on our childhood experiences as baby boomers in other midwestern places— northern Indiana and St. Louis. Tuna Noodle Casserole, we thought, and desserts made with rhubarb. We also kept an eye out for foods that might be especially important to Minnesota cooks, like blueberries, wild rice, and freshwater fish. Then to be sure we took a good look at midwestern community cookery outside Minnesota, we consulted cookbooks from our family collections, those of friends in other states, and the Szathmary Culinary Archives at the University of Iowa.

Reading the recipes reconnected us to wonderful memories. Tasting the samples was even more fun. We had three criteria for selection: the recipes had to taste good, they had to be something readers would cook and enjoy serving, and they had to be classics from midwestern 1950s kitchens. Our goal was to have our taste testers exclaim, "Oh, I remember that. I haven't had it in years. I should make it again."

Most of the recipes we've included here have appeared over and over again. St. Paul's version was essentially the same as the one from St. Louis. The one in the Swanington, Indiana, cookbook was close to the one from Hudson, South Dakota. These were common dishes in the 1950s, but most of them have disappeared from menus today. The recipes in this book are compilations of all of the versions and remain true to the ingredients and methods of the 1950s. However, as we worked our way through Swedish meatballs, Jell-O salads, and Snickerdoodles, we ran into a few surprises. We found some wonderful breads, pies, and main dishes neither one of us had seen before. We've included some of them and credited the authors.

Deb's ideas about midwestern cooking were formed in suburban St. Louis by a mother of Norwegian and German descent from Crystal Lake, Illinois, and a father who was 100 percent German, from Menasha and Madison, Wisconsin. After heading north to college and graduate school, she spent most of her adult life in Minnesota, with the exception of a year in Boston that was very educational both linguistically and culinarily. After a fortunate marriage to a native Minnesotan with Minnesota-born parents, she's learned from her mother-in-law about Minnesota cuisine in general (Swedish tea ring, seven-ingredient bars) and Iron Range South Slav eating in particular (*sarma*, or cabbage rolls, and *potitsa*, a kind of walnut strudel).

Rae grew up eating a "strictly American" melting pot cuisine on the Indiana side of Chicago. The several European heritages were so mixed up after generations of midwestern living as to be indistinguishable. Thankfully, midwestern roots are impossible to eradicate. Although life after graduation from the University of Iowa took Rae, husband, daughter, and son to various cities in Indiana, Illinois, Iowa—even Virginia, New Jersey, and Alabama—before landing in Minnesota, the Midwest was always home.

We feel lucky to be following *Hot Dish Heaven* and *Bundt Cake Bliss* to *Potluck Paradise*. We hope you enjoy the celestial kitchen journey.

ACKNOWLEDGMENTS

WE BOTH THANK GREG BRITTON, former director of the Minnesota Historical Society Press, for coming up with the idea for this cookbook. We thank Anne Kaplan, food scholar, taster, and cookbook guru, and Marilyn Ziebarth, our enthusiastic editor. Helen Newlin and Terri Hudoba helped produce the book for the press. Our taste testers at the press and in the Minnesota Historical Society reference and collections departments kept us going as they sampled and provided helpful feedback. (Now we know where that word comes from!) We owe a big thanks to Jane Monson, who pored over the midwestern community cookbooks at the University of Iowa's Szathmary Culinary Archives to find just what we needed, and some things we needed only after she had found them. *The authors*

Potluck Paradise could not have been written without Debbie Miller. Her generosity of spirit and expertise built the outstanding collection of community cookbooks at the historical society. We shared a lot of memories and laughs while we pored over batter-stained pages. Thanks to neighbors and friends who offered constructive comments, in particular Alice Twedt, who shared her good taste and collection of community cookbooks. As ever and always, my thanks to John, who keeps me in balance, samples countless test dishes, and lives with a household in controlled chaos during oh so many days of recipe refinement. *Rae Katherine Eighmey*

Working on *Potluck Paradise* with an experienced cook and cookbook writer like Rae has been great fun, gaining me both a co-author and a friend. Speaking of friends, I mustered the nerve to take on this project thanks to the support of two inspiring groups of women: my writing group, Marcia Anderson, Annette Atkins, and Anne Webb, and the Tackies, Annette Atkins, Jane Curry, Gretchen Kreuter, and Peg Meier. My thanks to Minnesota Historical Society acquisitions librarian Patrick Coleman for challenging me to investigate the world of Minnesota cookbooks. I thank my husband, BJ Lovegren, who's always game to eat and enjoy pretty much anything I cook, and his mom, Bunny Lovegren, who gave me such an expert introduction to mid-century Minnesota foods. I also thank my mom, Lu Miller, and my sister, Pat Miller, who have probably spent more time in the kitchen with me than anyone else on earth, starting in the 1950s and continuing through the recipe testing for this book. *Debbie Miller*

POTLUCK PARADISE

COMMUNITY COOKBOOKS

Debbie Miller

COOKBOOKS SPEAK TO ME. It's not just the recipes, but it would never happen without the recipes. Community cookbooks are the ones I mean, collections of everybody's best recipes from church and synagogue women's groups, American Legion auxiliaries and the Eastern Star, YWCAs and museums, hospitals, and orchestras. I've been collecting cookbooks for a long time, since my sixteenth birthday. For a special gift that year, my parents asked me what I would like. It wasn't hard to choose: Time-Life's Foods of the World cookbooks! A beautiful and practical set of books, the series featured for each country a large-format, full-color, gorgeously illustrated hardcover book and a small spiral-bound cardboard-covered recipes book that opened flat so cooks could easily use it. They could splatter on the little book without affecting the coffee-table beauty of the larger one. History and photographs and stories of the cooks in the big books drew me in. I was hooked. When I grew up, I tried to get a cookbook as a souvenir from the places I traveled. In Mexico in the 1980s I discovered Diana Kennedy's thoroughly researched and beautifully written books of recipes for Mexican foods. In Italy in 2006, I acquired an English translation of a lovely old Umbrian cookbook.

As a historian of Minnesota, I applied my cookbook interest to professional matters. How could the Minnesota Historical Society best document the many cookbooks published in the state over many decades? Encouraged to discover the universe of Minnesota cookbooks, I visited estate sales with a real purpose: to survey and acquire cookbooks of interest. It was an affordable hobby, since the books cost only $1 for hardcovers and 50 cents for paperbacks. Most of my favorites, the spiral-bound community cookbooks, had paper covers.

More than a thousand cookbooks later, I was able to describe the universe I'd had such fun discovering. No shooting stars or black holes here, just well-worn books with splattered pages and the occasional note, "Good!" or "Too sweet." Even after reading the carefully developed recipes in many Betty Crocker and Pillsbury cookbooks, the scrumptious recipes of the state's deservedly famous

3

Fabulous Finns, Bea Ojakangas and Elea-nor Ostman, the statewide compilations like the Best of Taste series from the Min-neapolis *Star,* and the Minnesota Histori-cal Society's cookbook compiled for the statehood centennial in 1958—my heart remains with the community cookbooks, or, as collectors call them, "charitable" cookbooks. They got that name because they're compiled and published to raise money for a church, synagogue, or other nonprofit group.

Most of the books are spiral bound, with a thin wire or wide plastic band looping through holes punched in the pages. (Nowadays the myriad of publish-ers of community cookbooks have moved to a plastic loose-leaf notebook. If any-thing, it's even more awkward to group on the bookshelf than the spirals, which do tend to catch on the spirals next door.) My very favorites, though, are the "home-made" cookbooks, typed and mimeo-graphed or thermofaxed, cut into pages with a paper cutter, covered with oilcloth or wallpaper samples cut out with a pink-ing shears, two or three holes punched in each page and cover, and finally "bound" with pipecleaners, yarn, or little gold-col-ored brads. In my experience, these are almost always church projects, books for which the women who made them did *all* the work and didn't have a printer or pub-lisher to pay afterwards before they could count their profits toward a new church furnace or painting the sanctuary.

The names of the 1950s-era books are comfortable and familiar: *Kitchen Favor-ites, Cooking with Our Friends, Come into Our Kitchens, Shared Recipes, The Mix-ing Bowl, Favorite Tested Recipes of [insert name here] Church, Adventures in the Kitchen, Kitchen Secrets.* Although their amateur status is part of their appeal, community cookbook compilers some-times called on home economists to offer insights into the daily chore and daily pleasure of cooking for the family. The women of Waverly Lutheran Church near Truman, Minnesota, recognized that Iowa home economist Bess Ferguson's ideas might inspire the cooks using their new cookbook, *Adventures in the Kitchen,* in 1954. In the introduction, Bess Ferguson sketched the joys of the beginning cook in a kitchen where expert help was at hand. "As I learned to cook, I began to real-ize that many of our favorite foods were made of the same things. The amounts we used and the way we put them together made the difference. Eggs, milk, sugar, and vanilla made a custard. Eggs, milk, sugar, and vanilla with some butter and flour made a cake. Now cooking was an adventure. I have been trying new recipes ever since."

Ferguson wrote engagingly about why we like to cook.

I believe it is because we like everything connected with food, how it tastes, how it smells and how it looks. We like the people we are cooking for, our families and friends. We like our old bowls—or our new ones, if we are young—and our mixing spoons, the whir-r-r of the beater. We like to collect recipes. Maybe we have been doing it for years, and the bulging boxes never get sorted but we go right on saving recipes scrawled on odds and ends of paper, recipes we picked up at the family reunion or copied out of a movie magazine at the beauty parlor.

Finally, Ferguson described *Adventures in the Kitchen* as Rae and Deb might describe this cookbook: "Here we have a cookbook, prepared BY women who like to cook, FOR women (and men!) who like to cook." Both books include family recipes, heirloom recipes from the old country, new and modern recipes, recipes for everyday meals, and recipes for company. Both books celebrate recipes of the 1950s Midwest, with an emphasis on Minnesota and the Upper Midwest.

We hope that reading and cooking from *Potluck Paradise* will lead you to read or reread your family's cookbooks from the 1950s and other decades to discover familiar recipes you remember from childhood. Finding the names of relatives and family friends under one of their favorite recipes can add spice to your search, and funny old advertisements that helped support printing of the books can make you smile.

Sometimes the women who compiled the community cookbooks speak directly from that time and place to us in our not-yet-familiar new millennium. The women of Waverly Lutheran began the section of their cookbook that discussed cooking for large groups with a charming essay highlighting the virtues of small-town life called "When We Cook for Company."

"Waverly folks are sociable," it begins. "Here the art of social calling is practiced at its gracious best. A neighbor family 'dropping in' for the evening, a family or two invited for supper, a family gathering for Sunday dinner after church, and the birthday party are most typical of Waverly hospitality. The most casual visitor does not leave without a cup of coffee." So of course each potential host family always has on hand a full cookie jar and a pantry of good things from which a quick supper—or at least "potluck"—can be assembled. Family potlucks, in the sense that everyone brings a dish to a gathering, get an enthusiastic endorsement here, especially for the benefit of young mothers. "Members of the family may take turns entertaining the clan for each of the holidays. In many families it is the practice for the host family to furnish the meat and potatoes with the other members co-operating on the rest of the meal. This is a happy situation for the hostess and makes it possible for even those with small children to entertain a large group quite easily."

May you encounter in *Potluck Paradise* recipes you remember eating, or hearing about. We hope you'll try many of them and that you'll like some of them enough to take to potlucks with your own family and friends, your book group or church supper. Whether you live in a small town or a big city, on a farm or a houseboat, the food-based sociability that the Minnesota women of Waverly Lutheran valued so greatly can enhance your life as well. Enjoy!

BREADS

Rae Katherine Eighmey

A neighbor once told me that she always baked a batch of bread when she was angry. She said she could work off a lot of ill feeling, punching and kneading the dough and when it came from the oven, brown and fragrant, she was proud of herself and no longer angry.

BESS FERGUSON, *ADVENTURES IN THE KITCHEN*,
WOMEN OF WAVERLY LUTHERAN CHURCH, TRUMAN, MN 1954

I sift this flour on my board.
It is so clean and good,
And, handling it, I am a part
Of all earth's womanhood.
For Women's hands have kneaded flour
To loaves since time began;
Each toiling for her own small brood,
Her own beloved man.

GOOD THINGS TO EAT, MARY AND MARTHA CIRCLE,
BETHESDA EVANGELICAL COVENANT CHURCH, ROCKFORD, IL

Many of our taste-testers say this is the best recipe in the book. It is also one of the cleverest quick bread recipes we've ever seen. The name says it all. Imagine the doorbell ringing on Sunday afternoon. Horrors! The Bishop has come to call and there isn't anything to offer him. Quick! Into the kitchen to throw together some sort of treat.

By combining the sugar, flour and shortening first, and setting some of that mixture aside, Ada R. Englund from Land's Lutheran Church in Hudson, South Dakota, made her streusel topping quickly, without messing up an additional bowl. And the Bishop got cake with his coffee.

Bishop's Bread

YIELD: 2 STANDARD LOAVES

1 tablespoon white vinegar

1 cup milk

2 cups flour

1½ cups brown sugar, firmly packed

½ teaspoon salt

½ cup cold butter or other shortening

1 teaspoon cinnamon

½ teaspoon baking soda

1 teaspoon baking powder

1 (8-ounce) package dates, chopped

1 cup chopped nuts

1 egg, lightly beaten

Preheat oven to 325°F. Grease two 8×4×4-inch loaf pans (see page 113 for tips). Combine the vinegar and milk and let stand until the milk sours, about 5 minutes. Mix flour, sugar and salt in a large mixing bowl. Cut in the butter or shortening with a pastry cutter until the mixture looks like cornmeal. Measure out ¼ cup and set it aside for the topping of the bread. Add cinnamon, baking soda and baking powder to the remaining flour mixture. Stir in the dates and nuts. Combine sour milk with the lightly beaten egg. Stir these liquid ingredients into the dry mixture until just blended. Divide the batter between loaf pans and sprinkle with the set-aside topping mixture. Bake until a skewer or knife poked into the center of the loaf comes out clean, about 50 to 60 minutes. If using a 13×9-inch cake pan, bake for 30 to 35 minutes.

BAKING PANS FOR THIS BREAD

Pan size influences how long breads or cakes take to bake. The larger the pan, the quicker it bakes. Ada didn't give a pan size in her original recipe but specified baking for "23 minutes." When we tested Bishop's Bread in loaf pans, this wasn't nearly long enough. If you bake it in a 13×9-inch pan it will take about that long, and the result is more of a coffee cake rectangle. I like being able to slice pieces off a loaf. Whatever pan you use, this is a wonderful adaptation of a 1950s standard date-nut bread.

Maraschino cherries lead a double life. By day, innocently sitting atop whipped cream, next to the nuts on hot fudge sundaes, or, more healthfully, on cottage cheese. But after the sun has passed the yardarm, these red charmers adopt an entirely new identity, skewered next to the orange slice on the swizzle stick after the bitters have been muddled with sugar and whisky in short glasses. At least that's my memory of how the ladies who played duplicate bridge in the 1950s celebrated the end of the afternoon's hands, savoring their Old Fashioneds before heading home to don aprons and make meatloaf.

About 1953 the maraschino cherry revealed a new talent in community cookbooks. The books we looked at contained a flurry of cherry nut bread recipes, giving this odd fruit yet another identity.

Cherry Nut Bread

YIELD: 5 MINI-LOAVES

1 (10-ounce) jar maraschino cherries, drained
  (reserve ¼ cup juice)
½ cup butter or other shortening
1¼ cups sugar
3 eggs
2 teaspoons baking powder
2½ cups flour
½ cup milk
1 teaspoon vanilla
chopped almonds or walnuts if desired

Preheat oven to 350°F. Grease 5 mini-loaf pans before baking (see page 113 for tips). Chop drained cherries roughly into quarters, and set aside. Cream butter and sugar. Stir in eggs and mix well. Add baking powder and half the flour. Stir in the milk, reserved cherry juice and vanilla, then the remaining flour. Fold in the nuts and chopped cherries. Divide batter among mini-loaf pans. Bake until breads pull away from the edges and a toothpick inserted in the center of the loaves comes out clean, about 40 to 45 minutes.

MARASCHINO CHERRIES

Sharon Herbst reports in the *Food Lover's Companion* that maraschino cherries get their name from Maraschino liquor, a sweet Italian drink made from wild cherries. In the past it was used as an ingredient in the pitted cherries. Now the cherries are artificially colored and typically steeped in sugar syrup flavored with almonds for red ones and mint for green.

hether at regular coffee klatches or just over the fence neighboring, housewives in the 1950s gathered for midmorning respite between chores. Someone would bring coffee cake, someone else muffins, and the hostess supplied the coffee. Quickly made breads were the foundation of these friendly gatherings.

Two foolproof methods for mixing these quick breads or coffee cakes are generously demonstrated in the pages of community cookbooks. Cranberry Bread combines the sifted dry with mixed wet ingredients. The Streusel Coffee Cake uses an electric mixer to beat the ingredients before layering with tasty brown sugar and cinnamon.

Cranberry Bread

YIELD: 1 LARGE LOAF

1 cup sugar

2 cups sifted flour

½ teaspoon salt

½ teaspoon baking soda

1 ½ teaspoons baking powder

1 cup diced cranberries (if frozen, dice before thawing)

½ cup chopped nuts (pecans or walnuts are good)

1 egg, lightly beaten

2 tablespoons melted butter or shortening

⅓ cup orange juice

grated rind of one orange

3 tablespoons hot water

Preheat oven to 350°F. Grease a large 9×5×4-inch loaf pan or 3 mini-loaf pans (see page 113 for tips). Sift sugar, flour, salt, baking soda and baking powder into a large mixing bowl. Stir in the cranberries and nuts. Combine egg, melted butter, orange juice, orange rind, and hot water. Quickly mix into the dry ingredients, stirring until just blended. Pour batter into pan and bake until a skewer inserted in the middle of the loaf comes out clean. Bake about 60 minutes for the large loaf pan or 45 minutes for mini-loaf pans.

Streusel Coffee Cake

YIELD: 1 COFFEE CAKE, SERVING 9

CAKE

1½ cups bread flour

2 teaspoons baking powder

½ teaspoon salt

¾ cup sugar

¼ cup softened butter or shortening

1 egg

¾ cup milk

1 teaspoon vanilla

FILLING (mix well with a fork)

½ cup brown sugar, firmly packed

2 tablespoons flour

2 teaspoons cinnamon

½ cup chopped pecans or other nuts

Preheat oven to 350°F. Combine cake ingredients in large mixing bowl and beat with electric mixer until very smooth. Put half of the batter in well-greased 9×9×2-inch pan; sprinkle with half of the filling. Cover with remaining batter and finally sprinkle last of filling mixture on top. Bake about 30 minutes, until light brown.

imple to make, easy to transport to the goodie-laden table and very popular sellers, quick breads and coffee cakes were the foundation of many a
successful fund-raising bake sale in the 1950s. Recipes for favored loaves
passed from homemaker to homemaker.

This cheese bread is one of the exceptional variations away from the typically sweet quick breads filling the pages of the cookbooks we examined. It's
well worth making even if you are trying to watch your cholesterol.

Cheese Bread

YIELD: 3 MINI-LOAVES

2 tablespoons white vinegar

1½ cups milk, or a little less

3 cups flour

1½ teaspoons baking soda

1 teaspoon salt

1½ cups grated sharp Cheddar cheese

1 teaspoon caraway seed (optional)

2 eggs, lightly beaten

¼ cup melted butter or shortening

Preheat oven to 350°F. Grease 3 mini-loaf pans before baking (see page 113 for
tips). Pour vinegar into a 2-cup glass measuring cup. Add enough milk to make
1½ cups. Stir and allow milk to sour, about 5 minutes. Combine flour, baking
soda, salt, cheese and optional caraway seeds in a large mixing bowl. Add sour
milk, eggs and melted butter and stir with a spoon until just blended. Pour
batter into mini-loaf pans. Bake until bread is firm in the center when tested
with a skewer and has pulled away from the sides of the pans, about 40 to 45
minutes. Cool on wire rack for 10 minutes; remove from pans and continue to
cool with the bread on its side for several hours before slicing.

BAKING WITH SOUR MILK

Not so very long ago cooks would look at the glass bottle filled with lumpy curdled milk not as a candidate for the disposal but as an essential ingredient. The magic interaction of sour milk with baking soda makes lots of  bubbles, resulting in nicely raised breads and cakes. Today, cooks generally don't have sour milk about in the fridge, so we need to sour our own. I usually just use one tablespoon of white vinegar to a cup of milk, or so. Adding too much vinegar will sour the milk—but the balance of sour to soda will be off and the resulting baked good will have an off taste as well. You can also use lemon juice in the same proportion. Whatever method you use, don't shilly-shally about getting the batter into the oven once you've mixed it up. The quicker you bake it, the more bubbles you will capture.

This Swedish bread has a wonderful hint of orange and anise to complement the usual rye bread caraway seeds. The dough is heavy, so allow plenty of time for it to rise.

Swedish Limpa

YIELD: 2 (6-INCH) ROUND LOAVES

1½ cups water
½ cup brown sugar, firmly packed
2 teaspoons caraway seed
1 tablespoon butter or shortening
1 tablespoon grated orange rind
1 package instant rapid rise yeast
½ cup warm water
1 tablespoon sugar
3 cups white bread flour, plus up to 1 cup additional
2 cups rye flour
1 teaspoon anise seed

Combine 1½ cups water, brown sugar, caraway seed, butter and orange rind in a medium saucepan. Bring to a boil over medium heat and cook for 3 minutes. Remove from heat and let cool to lukewarm (about 100°F). Pour into a large mixing bowl. Combine the yeast with the ½ cup warm water and sugar. In a few minutes the mixture should start foaming as the yeast proofs. Add this to mixing bowl. Stir in the 3 cups bread flour with a spoon until thoroughly blended. Cover top of the bowl with plastic wrap and set in a warm place to rise until double; this could take 2 hours. Stir the dough down and add 2 cups rye flour and the anise seed. Add additional bread flour until you have a dough that isn't sticky. Knead until smooth. Put dough into a clean bowl, cover with plastic wrap and let rise until doubled again; this could take another 2 hours. Punch down dough. Form into two round loaves. Place them on lightly greased baking sheets and allow to rise until double once again; this might only take another hour. Bake in a preheated 350°F oven until the tops are lightly browned and the bread sounds hollow when tapped, about 40 minutes. Cool on a wire rack.

WORKING WITH YEAST DOUGH

I usually make breads using instant yeast. Being impatient, I also use the quick-rise type. Whatever kind of yeast you use, the methods are the same. Yeast is a living organism. It makes bread rise by producing gas that is trapped in the elastic gluten of bread flour, stretching it to enclose the bubbles. Always make sure the yeast will do its job by "proofing" it. Combine the yeast with warm water and a bit of sugar for it to eat. If the mixture gets foamy, you'll know your bread will too. Be patient and careful. If the proofing water or ingredients are too hot, you will kill the yeast. 100°F is a good temperature. It should feel slightly warm on the inside of your wrist. Once mixed, the dough needs a warm place to rise as well. But heat kills there, too. Or too cold, and the yeast will just take a nap. It's hard to say how long any particular recipe will take to rise. Both temperature and the "oomph" of the yeast you are using make a tremendous difference. If you allow a half day to make most breads and rolls in this book, you should be fine. With a bit of practice you'll get a feel for the proper elasticity of the kneaded dough. Whole wheat and rye flours are heavier and have less gluten. Breads made from them need more time to rise before baking. Yeast breads are really simple to make. Be kind and gentle to your yeast and it will reward you with lovely light loaves.

rank Ferguson grew up in Ames, Iowa. His mother, Bess, shared recipes and advice with central Iowa women as a radio homemaker on WOI during the 1950s. Frank remembers Bess bringing this coffee cake to his high school play rehearsals. Essentially it is a rich cinnamon roll. The trick of forming the dough into a ring and then alternating the partially sliced rolls to the inside and outside of the dough ring made this an elegant refreshment for ladies' club meetings as well as a filling one for the needs of starving teenaged thespians.

Swedish Tea Ring

YIELD: 2 LARGE COFFEE CAKE RINGS, EACH SERVING 12

1 cup milk

½ cup plus 1 tablespoon sugar, divided

1 teaspoon salt

2 packages instant yeast

¼ cup lukewarm water

5 to 6 cups bread flour

2 eggs, lightly beaten

¼ cup melted shortening or butter, cooled

FILLING:

1 stick butter, melted

⅔ cup brown sugar, divided

2 teaspoons cinnamon, divided

GLAZE:

1 tablespoon melted butter

2 tablespoons cream

1 cup confectioner's sugar

½ teaspoon vanilla

chopped nuts, optional

Scald the cup of milk in a saucepan, heating until small bubbles form around the side. Add ½ cup of the sugar and salt. Stir gently until they are dissolved. Set aside to cool. Combine yeast and 1 tablespoon of the sugar with warm water and set aside until it becomes bubbly. Place cooled scalded milk in a large mixing bowl. Add 2 cups of the bread flour and mix with a wooden spoon. Add dissolved yeast, eggs and cooled melted shortening. Add more flour until you have a soft dough that isn't sticky. Knead on a lightly floured surface until the dough is smooth and elastic, about 5 minutes.

Place dough in a clean, lightly greased bowl, cover with a damp cloth and set in a warm place so it can rise until doubled, about an hour. Punch down and divide dough into two pieces. Roll each piece into a rectangle ½-inch thick and about 20×12 inches on a lightly floured surface. Brush with melted butter and sprinkle ⅛ cup of the brown sugar and 1 teaspoon of the cinnamon. Roll from the long side jelly-roll fashion.

Place on a lightly greased cookie sheet and form the roll into a circle. With scissors, make cuts 1 inch apart through the top of the ring to within an inch from the bottom. Fan cut slices, bringing one to the center and one to the outside, twisting them slightly to lay flat on the sheet. Repeat with remaining dough. Let rise until double in size, about a half hour. Preheat oven to 375°F. Bake for 20 to 25 minutes until lightly browned. Remove from oven and cool slightly. Mix glaze ingredients and drizzle over the top of the tea ring while it is still warm. Sprinkle with chopped nuts if desired.

Yeast casserole breads are easy to make. No kneading necessary. Just a brisk stirring is enough to stretch the gluten. The cooked onion and egg topping on this bread gives it rich sophistication. Be sure to put the casserole on a cookie sheet while baking, just in case a bit of the topping slips off.

Casserole Onion Bread

YIELD: 1 LARGE ROUND LOAF

BREAD

1 cup milk

1½ tablespoons shortening or butter

1 teaspoon onion salt

½ teaspoon celery salt

2 packages instant dry yeast

3 tablespoons sugar

1 cup warm water

4½ cups bread flour

TOPPING

2 tablespoons butter

¾ cup chopped onion

1 egg yolk

1 teaspoon water

Scald the cup of milk in a saucepan, heating until small bubbles form around the side. Add shortening, onion salt and celery salt. Stir until dissolved and set aside until cooled to lukewarm. Combine yeast and sugar with warm water. Stir and set aside until bubbly. Put flour into large bowl. Add milk and yeast mixtures, stirring until well blended, about 2 minutes. Cover with a damp towel and set aside to rise in a warm place until tripled in bulk, about 45 minutes.

Preheat oven to 375°F. Stir the batter down and beat by hand vigorously about a half minute. Lightly grease a 2-quart round casserole dish about 8½ inches in diameter and 3 inches high. Pour batter into casserole, place on a baking sheet and bake on a rack just below the center of the oven.

While the bread is baking, make the onion topping. Melt butter over low heat in a frying pan. Add chopped onion, stir and cover. Cook about 5 minutes until tender. Cool. Beat the egg yolk with a fork or whisk in a small bowl until light, about a minute. Add the water and blend well. Then stir in the cooked onions. When the bread is set, but not completely baked—about 40 minutes—spoon onion mixture evenly over the top of the loaf. Bake an additional 20 minutes until top is golden brown. Remove from oven. Let cool for 10 minutes, then turn out of casserole and flip to cool with onion mixture on top.

> No one who cooks, cooks alone.
> Even at her most solitary, a cook
> in the kitchen is surrounded by
> generations of cooks past, the
> advice and menus of cooks present,
> the wisdom of cookbook writers.
>
> **LAURIE COLWIN**

RELISHES and SALADS

Rae Katherine Eighmey

If it is vanity, this taking pride
In ruffled curtains, newly ironed,
Of these gold spheres of pickled apricots inside
Their jars, or currant jelly, forgive me, please.

If it is wrong, this looking proudly toward
The table cover made with one's own hand,
Or silver polished bright, forgive me, Lord—
But I am sure You smile, and understand.

GOOD THINGS TO EAT, MARY AND MARTHA CIRCLE,
BETHESDA EVANGELICAL COVENANT CHURCH, ROCKFORD, IL

*R*elish is a wonderful word. It carries with it the tasty expectation of a deliciously prepared and enjoyable meal. The relish that Mrs. A. Larson of Norwegian Lutheran Memorial Church in Minneapolis shared is a wonderful combination. It is a variation of the typical "end of garden" relishes that combine tomatoes, peppers, whatever else can be tossed into the pickle. The apples Mrs. Larson added to the mix make all the difference. This is lightly flavored and provides a tart accent to whatever is next to it on the plate. It is equally at home on top of a hot dog, sparking up a plate of lentils or providing a counterpoint to a bacon-wrapped filet.

Lick'um Good Relish

YIELD: ABOUT 4 PINTS

4 large tart apples, peeled and cored

4 medium mild onions, peeled

4 ripe tomatoes, peeled and seeded

1 green bell pepper, seeded

½ red bell pepper, seeded

1 cup sugar

1 cup vinegar

1 tablespoon salt

¼ teaspoon ground allspice

Dice and process the apples, onions, tomatoes and peppers in a food processor or put through a food chopper so that the pieces are about ⅛-inch in size. Put into a large stock pot. Add the remaining ingredients and bring to a simmer over medium heat. Cook for 30 minutes after the relish begins to simmer, stirring from time to time. Pour into sterilized canning jars, top with a sterilized canning lid and process in a boiling water bath according to USDA guidelines (at this writing 15 minutes for pints and 10 minutes for half pints). Or keep in refrigerator for up to a month.

PUTTING FOOD UP

If you have never canned, it isn't all that hard. Safe canning requires cleanliness, attention to detail, and a lot of hot water. Times have changed since our grandmothers put up jams and jellies in whatever glass jars they had and sealed them with a half-inch layer of paraffin. We've given procedures for canning in this recipe, but the U.S. Department of Agriculture is continually reevaluating home canning procedures. (Check their Web site or that of the National Center for Home Food Preservation at the University of Georgia for the latest safe-practice guidance.)

Small batches will keep in the refrigerator for a few weeks. I always sterilize the jars if I'm going to keep relish or jam for more than a week in the fridge. Use jars designed for home canning. Put them in a large pot and fill it with hot water so that the entire jar is under at least an inch of water. Bring the water to a full rolling boil and boil for 20 minutes. It is a good idea to drop the lids in boiling water for 3 minutes as well. Any product that I'm going to keep on the shelf or in the refrigerator for longer than a month I process in a boiling water bath according to the USDA guidelines.

This recipe was in every cookbook we opened. It had a few different names: 12-Hour Salad, 24-Hour Salad, Overnight Salad are just a few. I must admit I was skeptical of the marshmallows. They are not my favorite food. But overnight the flavors mellow to make this a perfect "fancy" salad. Just right for impressing the boss. The '50s homemaker would have done all the hard work the day before so she could don her prettiest dress and frilly apron and serve the individual salad plates modestly saying, "Oh, it's nothing—I hope you enjoy it," while the Chicken Tremendous bakes in the oven.

Millionaire's Salad

SERVES 10

2 (14-to-16-ounce) cans Queen Anne white cherries, halved

2 (8-ounce) cans diced pineapple

2 (14-to-16-ounce) cans Mandarin oranges

2 cups quartered marshmallows or miniature ones

¼ pound blanched, slivered almonds

DRESSING

2 eggs

2 tablespoons sugar

¼ cup light cream

juice of one lemon

1 cup heavy cream, whipped

Drain cherries, pineapple, and oranges. Combine with marshmallows and almonds. Next make the dressing. Beat eggs until light, gradually add sugar, light cream and lemon juice. Mix thoroughly, and cook in double boiler until smooth and thick, stirring constantly. Remove from heat and cool. Pour over fruit mixture. Cover tightly and chill 12 to 24 hours in refrigerator. Stir just before serving and gently fold in whipped cream. Serve on crisp lettuce leaf.

When summer gardens faded under falling leaves, fresh salads in the 1950s largely vanished as well. Canned vegetables freshened with tangy vinegar sauce made a good potluck stand-in for the summer fresh cucumber salad. This vegetable version of a 24-hour salad is a family favorite at our house winter and summer. It keeps in the refrigerator for three to five days. You can even leave the oil out of the dressing if you want to cut calories.

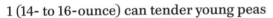

24-Hour Vegetable Salad

SERVES 6 TO 8

1 (14- to 16-ounce) can tender young peas

1 (14- to 16-ounce) can French cut green beans

1 (14- to 16-ounce) can shoepeg (sweet) white corn

4 large stalks celery, diced

1 can pimento, cut fine

1 medium onion, diced

1 green pepper, diced

1 cup sugar

1 teaspoon paprika

1 teaspoon salt

1 cup vinegar

½ cup vegetable oil

Drain and mix vegetables in a large, heatproof bowl. Combine sugar, paprika and salt in a saucepan. Add vinegar, stirring to dissolve sugar. Bring mixture to a boil over medium heat and pour while hot over the combined vegetables. Stir to mix well and add the vegetable oil. Refrigerate overnight.

This book wouldn't be complete without Jell-O salads—a key midwestern food group. Interestingly, cooks in different states appear to prefer different colors for their Jell-O salads. North Dakotans like red, Iowans have a slight preference for orange, and Minnesotans use either lemon or lime. Our personal taste preferences kept us from even considering the entire world of cottage cheese congealed in lime Jell-O. These two versions passed taste tests with flying colors.

Golden Glow Salad

SERVES 6

1 (3-ounce) package lemon Jell-O
1 cup boiling water
1 cup canned pineapple juice
1 tablespoon vinegar
⅓ cup pineapple, diced and drained
1 cup finely grated carrots
⅓ cup pecans, chopped fine
½ teaspoon salt
mayonnaise for topping, if desired

Dissolve Jell-O in boiling water. Add pineapple juice and chill until slightly thickened. Then add vinegar, diced pineapple, carrots, pecans and salt. As the Jell-O sets, stir gently until ingredients are evenly distributed. Pour into a square or loaf pan or mold. Chill until firm. Serve on lettuce and topped with a dab of mayonnaise.

Apricot Pineapple Jell-O

SERVES 12

2 (3-ounce) packages lemon Jell-O

1⅓ cups boiling water

1⅓ cups cold water

1 (14-to 16-ounce) can apricots, drained and mashed,
    reserving juice for topping

1 (14-to 16-ounce) can crushed pineapple, drained,
    reserving juice for topping

miniature marshmallows, optional

Dissolve Jell-O in boiling water. Add cold water, apricots and pineapple. Pour into a 12×9-inch pan and place in refrigerator. Stir from time to time to evenly distribute fruit until the Jell-O begins to set. If you want to use the marshmallows, arrange them on the top when the Jell-O is nearly set.

TOPPING

½ cup reserved apricot juice

½ cup reserved pineapple juice

½ cup sugar

1 egg, lightly beaten

2 tablespoons butter

2 tablespoons flour

1 cup heavy cream, whipped, or 1 (8-ounce) container Cool Whip, thawed

Combine the reserved juices, sugar, egg, butter and flour in a medium sauce pan. Cook and stir over low heat for 5 minutes, until the sugar and flour are dissolved and the mixture is slightly thickened. Cool completely and then fold in the whipped cream. Spread over the set Jell-O and return to the refrigerator until ready to serve.

had not planned on doing any canning this summer, and I certainly wasn't going berry-picking as I'd done in other years. I figured I'd get a quart of berries at the supermarket and that would work out fine to test this recipe. But this year was a very, very good strawberry year at Furleigh's U-Pick farm on Old Highway 18 between Mason City and Clear Lake, Iowa. The Fareway grocery is a bit farther west on the highway and so Furleigh's takes extra berries to sell there too.

On Saturday, just after the first day of summer, the 8-foot square table in the center of the Fareway produce section was stacked high with plastic-wrapped two-quart boxes heaped to nearly overflowing with impeccable strawberries. The aroma escaping through the folds of plastic stopped me in my tracks with its seductive perfume. Once you've preserved or pickled something—anything—it is nearly impossible to walk away from affordable bounty.

Which is how the 8 quarts of strawberries ended up in my cart. Oh, yes, and the 10-pound sack of sugar. Sunday evening back up in St. Paul my kitchen counters were arrayed with pots and bowls of sugaring down berries. The canner kettle was boiling, sterilizing pint jars. Over the next hours, batch after 20-minute batch was boiled, simmered, skimmed and sealed. By the time the long Minnesota early summer twilight faded, ruby-colored jars of preserves lined my now-clean counters.

The glass measuring cup held the last half cup that wouldn't fit in a jar. Why bother with a spoon? I plucked out a perfect berry, and then another and another. I had forgotten how good these preserves are. They were my mother-in-law's favorite. The sugar draws out the natural juices while keeping the berries intact as they float in a light syrup.

Early August found me down to the last two jars. Why did I share so many with friends? I saved the slightly thickened syrupy juice and will freeze it for winter pancakes. I planned to be back in Iowa the next weekend, but, alas, the season has ended for Furleigh's strawberry crop.

Strawberry Preserves

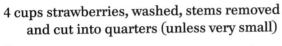

YIELD: 6 CUPS

4 cups strawberries, washed, stems removed
   and cut into quarters (unless very small)

5 cups sugar

Sprinkle the sugar over the berries and let stand for 2 hours at room temperature. Stir from time to time as the strawberries yield juice. After 2 hours, put the mixture into a large pot and slowly bring to a boil. Reduce heat, but keep at a slow boil, and cook for 10 minutes. Remove from heat and skim off any white foam. Pour preserves into sterilized jars and process according to USDA guidelines. Or keep preserves in the refrigerator for up to a month.

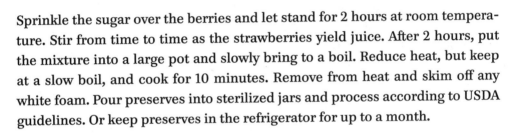

POTLUCK PRESERVES

Now that I've rediscovered this method, I've used it several time to preserve odd bits of soft fruit that might have ended up in the compost. Cutting the good parts from damaged peaches, old pears, slightly wrinkled apricots, sugaring them down and boiling for 10 minutes makes a lovely little jar.

Sharp vinegar-steeped vegetables are essential for summer meals. One woman who sent in a cucumber salad recipe pointed out that it was "good for summer picnics." That it is. No mayonnaise to worry about spoiling. These salads are good in the winter too. The cucumbers and onions pile up very nicely next to any kind of rich meat, especially ham.

As for the coleslaw—of course it's a great picnic dish. Try it in a sandwich, too, on rye with Swiss and warm corned beef. Can't be beat!

Cucumber Salad

SERVES 7 TO 8

1 large cucumber
2 medium onions
½ cup sugar
½ cup vinegar
½ teaspoon salt

Select a cucumber that has not been coated with wax to preserve it. Wash thoroughly and slice the unpeeled cucumber and onions as thin as possible, about a 1/16 of an inch. Put slices into a heatproof bowl. Combine the sugar, vinegar and salt in a small saucepan. Bring to a boil, stirring to completely dissolve the sugar. Pour this boiling dressing over the vegetables and stir. Cover and bring to room temperature, then put in refrigerator to chill before serving. This will keep in the refrigerator up to a week.

Super Coleslaw

SERVES 6

1 teaspoon salt

¼ teaspoon pepper

½ teaspoon dry mustard

1 teaspoon celery salt

2 tablespoons sugar

1 tablespoon chopped pimento

⅛ teaspoon grated onion

3 tablespoons vegetable oil

⅛ cup vinegar

¼ cup diced green pepper

3 cups finely shredded cabbage

Place ingredients in a large bowl in the order given. Mix well. Cover and chill for at least 2 hours before serving.

MAIN DISHES

Rae Katherine Eighmey

Shed a tear for the succulent roast or chop
That comes to the table a burnt-up flop
Because a gal with a frying-pan
Thought any old meat would please her man.
Then give a cheer for the smart little cook
Who studies the pages of this here book
And turns out a dish of which he's fond.
Worthy of serving Chateaubriand.

*SYMPHONY OF COOKING, WOMEN'S ASSOCIATION OF THE
ST. LOUIS SYMPHONY SOCIETY, ST. LOUIS, MO (1954)*

idwestern rivers and lakes have provided tasty fish for supper as long as people have been on the land. Lake cottages and resorts provide opportunities for relaxation and recreation. These two forces combine year after year in the experiences of visitors, creating a home of the heart and relaxation for the soul. So powerful can this experience be that it is enough to name a recipe after the resort "home" to maintain ties all year round. Perhaps that is why Mrs. Frank Cullman of Dallas, Texas, sent in a recipe to the Alexandria Lake Vacation Region cookbook for her fish dish named after that west-central Minnesota lake town.

Fish Alexandria

SERVES 4

4 fish steaks or thick fillets, any type you like
Salt and pepper to taste
3 tablespoons butter
½ cup whole milk
4 slices crisply cooked bacon
8 tomato halves, broiled

Preheat oven to 350°F. Sprinkle the fish with salt and pepper. Melt butter in a frying pan, add the fish and brown on both sides. Place fish on an ovenproof baking dish, pour milk over and bake until flaking, 5 to 15 minutes, depending on type and thickness of the fish. While fish are baking, cook bacon in frying pan and drain on paper towels. To serve, put bacon on fish and surround with broiled tomatoes.

I admit it. I grew up in the big city and prefer my fish to come from the end of a grocery line instead of a fishing line. However you bring home the catch, this simple preparation makes a well-flavored fish without adding fat or worrying about smelling up the house—it is the perfect definition of a Shore Lunch delivered in the back yard. The original directions called for cooking on a grill, but the foil would protect the fish and seasonings equally well in an oven or nestled in the ebbing coals of a lakeside campfire.

Walleye Pike in Foil

YIELD: 1 FISH FOR EACH PERSON

walleye, whole or fillets
salt
lemon slices
onion slices
bay leaf, discard before serving
thyme

Build a medium to low fire in your grill. Have a piece of heavy-duty foil large enough to wrap the fish securely. Place the fish on the foil. If whole, place the seasonings inside the fish. If a fillet, place the fish skin side down and put seasonings on top of it. Sprinkle each piece of fish lightly with salt. Then place a thin slice of lemon, one of onion, small piece of bay leaf and a pinch of thyme on the fish. Wrap the fish in the foil and seal both ends carefully. Place on grate for about 8 minutes for fillets. Turn a whole fish over to cook from the other side for another 8 minutes. Open package carefully! Hot steam will be trapped inside.

Simple or gussied up, combinations of macaroni and cheese are an essential midwestern food group. Grandsons Justin and Jack nuke after-school mac and cheese in less than three minutes. Taste testing these recipes demonstrated that it is well worth the effort to take some time with these pantry basics.

Plain and simple, this easy recipe yields a subtle contemplation of macaroni AND cheese. Without the typical cheese-laden white sauce, each ingredient stands on its own. The type of cheese you use makes a difference. Sharp cheddar produces chewy, cheesy bits; Colby or Jack are a bit mellower; and processed American is the creamiest. Although not found in the 1950s, today's whole wheat macaroni noodles give a nice nutty flavor.

Macaroni and Cheese

SERVES 4 AS A MAIN COURSE, 8 AS A SIDE DISH

1 (8-ounce) package elbow macaroni

16 ounces cheddar, Colby or processed American cheese, chopped into ¼-inch cubes

½ teaspoon freshly ground pepper

1¾ cup milk

Preheat oven to 425°F. Cook macaroni in boiling water until just tender. Do not overcook. Drain. Lightly grease a 2-quart casserole. Place about ⅓ of the macaroni in the bottom of the casserole, pepper it lightly and then cover with ⅓ of the cheese cubes. Repeat layers twice more, ending with the cheese. Put casserole in oven for 10 minutes. Then pour the milk over the top and stir gently. Reduce the oven temperature to 325°F and bake until the cheese is melted and bubbly, about 50 minutes. Stir carefully once or twice during baking.

My mother-in-law fed two voracious teenaged boys with this on a weekly basis. She made it in her electric frying pan, adding the macaroni, juice and cheese to the browned meat and simmering with the cover on and vent opened. If you don't still have your electric skillet (or your grandmother's), the oven-baked version is just as good.

Goulash

SERVES 4 TO 6 (OR 2 FAMISHED TEENAGED BOYS)

1 (8-ounce) package elbow macaroni
8 ounces ground beef
1 medium onion, diced
1 green pepper, diced
1 (24-ounce) can tomato juice
6 ounces cheddar or American cheese, cubed

To prepare in electric frying pan on counter top. (For oven preparation, preheat oven to 325°F and lightly grease a 12×9-inch baking dish.) Cook macaroni in boiling water until slightly underdone, drain and set aside. Crumble the ground beef into electric skillet on medium heat. (For oven preparation, use a frying pan over medium heat.) As the meat begins to brown, add the diced onion and green pepper. Cook until the onion is transparent. Drain off fat and add macaroni, tomato juice and cheese, stirring so the ingredients are evenly distributed. Cover with lid, lower temperature to 300°F. Cook until the macaroni has absorbed the tomato juice and the cheese is melted, about 30 minutes. (For oven preparation, put ingredients into baking dish, stir, cover with foil and bake about 30 minutes.)

sk any one of us over a certain age and you'll hear sagas of Basic Meals in Rotation, combinations of entrées and side dishes that were our mother's go-to dinners. Among the favorites—spaghetti with hamburger tomato sauce, iceberg lettuce salad, and garlic bread; ham, creamed new potatoes, and peas; or pork chops, applesauce, mashed potatoes, and pan gravy. Pretty standard dishes, solid, nutritious, boring. Homemakers who contributed to community cookbooks sent in variations of those classics, still using some combinations and everyday ingredients, but in innovative ways.

Pork Chops in Catsup Sauce

SERVES 6

¼ cup catsup

1 teaspoon yellow mustard

1 teaspoon salt

6 pork chops

2 tablespoons shortening or vegetable oil

8 ounces pitted prunes

½ teaspoon cinnamon

⅛ teaspoon ground cloves

1 cup water

¼ cup honey

1 tablespoon vinegar

Combine the catsup, mustard and salt. Brush mixture onto pork chops. Heat shortening or oil in frying pan that has a lid. Brown chops on both sides over medium heat. While chops are browning, combine remaining ingredients in a saucepan and bring to a boil. Lower heat and simmer until prunes are plumped. Pour prune sauce over chops, cover and simmer until chops are done, about 20 to 30 minutes depending on thickness.

I have to confess I never mourned the disappearance of the baked lima bean or butter bean from my diet. Frankly, I hadn't even thought about them for years. To put it bluntly, more than a few "starving children in other parts of the world" discussions took place at the dinner table over the baked butter bean. But looking at this recipe with a more adult palate and nutritional sensibility, the memory of these beans kind of warmed up. I figured it was worth a test. "Doctoring up" beans for this dish with onions, brown sugar, corn syrup and cream makes them really good.

Baked Lima Beans

SERVES 4 TO 6

1 pound dried lima beans, or 2 (14- to 16-ounce) cans lima beans or butter beans

1 medium onion, diced

1 teaspoon salt (optional)

1 tablespoon brown sugar

1 tablespoon dark corn syrup

1 tablespoon vinegar

1 cup cream

If using dried beans, follow the soaking directions on the package. If starting with canned, drain and rinse them well. Preheat oven to 350°F. Lightly grease a 2-quart casserole dish with a cover. Put in the drained lima beans. Add onion, optional salt, brown sugar, corn syrup and vinegar. Stir until mixed. Bake beans for 1 hour with the cover on. Add cream, stir and bake one hour longer until beans are very tender and sauce is slightly thickened. Remove the cover for the last 20 minutes.

H am is not a meat that falls onto the grill every day. This recipe from the early days of modern home grilling is deceptively simple and well worth reviving, as is the technique of slow cooking and gentle basting so that the glaze builds on the meat. Variations of the ham loaf that follows appeared in almost every cookbook we read.

Barbecued Ham Slices

SERVES 6

2 pounds ham slices, pre-cooked, about 1-inch thick

SAUCE
¾ cup water
1 cup catsup
2 tablespoons Worcestershire sauce
3 tablespoons cider vinegar
1 large onion, minced
dash of cloves
dash of cinnamon
salt and pepper to taste

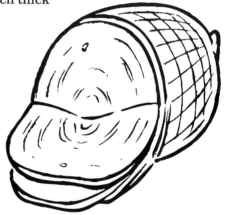

Combine the sauce ingredients. Build a slow to medium fire in your grill. Lay ham slices on the grill and brush with sauce. Because the ham is already cooked the grilling process heats the meat and infuses it with sauce. Watch carefully, turn and baste frequently. If the fire is low enough this will produce a nicely glazed piece of ham. The original directions suggest cooking 15 to 20 minutes. Grilling time will depend on the heat of your coals and how far the grill is above them.

Baked Ham Loaf

SERVES 6 TO 8

HAM LOAF

1½ pounds ground ham

1 pound lean ground pork

2 beaten eggs

½ cup milk

⅛ teaspoon pepper

1 cup finely crushed cracker crumbs

pineapple rings and cherries for garnish, if desired

GLAZE

1½ cups brown sugar

1 tablespoon prepared mustard

½ cup water

½ cup vinegar

SAUCE

1 cup whipping cream

1 tablespoon horseradish

1 tablespoon mustard

Preheat oven to 350°F. Combine the loaf ingredients and place in a loaf pan or casserole. Garnish with pineapple rings and maraschino cherries, if desired. Bake 1½ hours. Combine glaze ingredients and brush on loaf during the last half hour. Remove loaf from oven and let stand for 10 minutes before slicing. While the loaf is resting, whip cream until soft peaks form and then fold in the horseradish and mustard. Serve sauce on the side.

The world was a lot simpler when evening news programs were fifteen minutes long. Or at least it seemed that way. There were countries and even entire continents that Walter Cronkite or Huntley and Brinkley didn't mention. Newspapers in the town where I grew up emphasized local news and politics. But food helps make powerful connections. I was surprised that a real international story, one I had completely forgotten, popped into my head when I saw these recipes for Hungarian Cauliflower and Chicken Paprikosh. The Hungarian uprising of 1956 may have been the first time I ever paid attention to something happening overseas.

Hungarian Cauliflower

SERVES 6 TO 8

1 large head cauliflower or about 4 cups florets
1 cup sour cream
¼ to ½ cup milk
1 cup dried bread crumbs
2 tablespoons melted butter
butter for greasing baking dish

If using a whole cauliflower, remove the leaves and core and divide into florets, about 2×1 inches. Cook cauliflower in simmering water until tender. While the cauliflower is cooking, preheat oven to 350°F. Drain cauliflower and arrange evenly in a lightly greased 12×9-inch baking dish. Thin the sour cream with enough milk so that you can pour it over the cauliflower. Combine the bread crumbs and melted butter, then sprinkle over the top. Bake until cream is bubbly and bread crumbs are browned, about 20 to 30 minutes.

Chicken Paprikosh with Dumplings

SERVES 4 TO 6

1 medium onion, peeled and chopped

1 green pepper, seeded and chopped

2 tablespoons vegetable oil

2 teaspoons sweet imported Hungarian paprika

1 3-pound chicken, cut in pieces

1 large fresh tomato, seeded and chopped,
    or 1 (14- to 16-ounce) can diced tomatoes, drained

½ to 1 pint sour cream

chopped parsley for garnish

In a large frying pan with a lid, sauté the onion and green pepper in oil over medium heat until the onion is transparent. Sprinkle the paprika over the mixture and stir for a minute. Add the chicken pieces and cook until lightly browned. Add tomato, turn heat to very low, cover and simmer for about 45 minutes. Do not add water, but watch carefully so that it doesn't burn. When chicken is done, remove to serving dish. Stir sour cream into frying pan to make the sauce. To serve: Pour sauce over chicken, top with dumplings and sprinkle with parsley.

DUMPLINGS

1 egg

½ cup flour

¼ cup or less water as needed to make batter
    that can be dropped from a spoon

Bring a quart of water to a boil in a large pot or deep frying pan. Blend egg with flour and very gradually add enough water to make batter. Drop by teaspoons into boiling water a few at a time. Cover and let simmer for 7 minutes.

Rice and wild rice, especially in Minnesota and Wisconsin, helped stretch many a meat course. We found dozens of versions of these two rice dishes. They passed our taste tests with flying colors. The women who made these embellished rice dishes certainly would have dodged the dreaded potluck dinner nightmare—a still-full dish on the buffet table. They gleefully would have toted home an empty casserole.

Wild Rice Dish

SERVES 8

½ cup butter

½ pound sliced mushrooms

1 clove garlic, minced

1 cup well-washed wild rice

2 tablespoons minced chives
   or green onion tops

2 tablespoons minced green pepper

½ cup slivered almonds

3 cups chicken broth

Preheat oven to 350°F. Melt the butter in a large frying pan over medium heat. Add mushrooms and garlic. Cook, stirring frequently, until mushrooms are tender. Add wild rice and cook until grains are coated with butter and have browned slightly, about 5 minutes. Stir in chives, green pepper and almonds. Spoon mixture into a 2-quart casserole and slowly add chicken broth. Give mixture a stir, cover and bake until rice is tender, about 60 to 90 minutes.

The original recipe suggested serving with a cream sauce. But our taste testers thought it was fine just as it is.

ST. LOUIS VARIATION: Cook one cup of wild rice in water according to package directions. Combine with one cup white sauce and bake for 45 to 60 minutes at 325°F.

Green Rice Casserole

SERVES 6 TO 8

3 eggs, separated

2 cups cooked white rice

1 cup grated sharp cheese

¼ cup melted butter

salt and pepper to taste

2 tablespoons chopped onion

1 cup chopped parsley

butter for greasing baking dish

Preheat oven to 350°F. Beat egg whites until they form stiff peaks and set aside. Combine remaining ingredients including egg yolks, mixing thoroughly. Fold beaten egg whites into mixture. Bake in a well-greased 9×9-inch baking dish until mixture is firm in the center, about 25 minutes. Cut into squares and serve with creamed crab, shrimp or other meat.

COOKING RICE

Cooking rice is a process of slow encouragement. Each grain needs time, heat and liquid enough to swell and soften, but not so much as to get sticky and gooey. Begin with careful measurement of liquid and rice. If your package has recommendations, use them. My rule of thumb is 1 cup white or brown rice to 2 cups liquid. For white rice I bring the liquid to a boil, stir in the rice, put on a lid and reduce the heat to low. Simmer for 20 minutes. Brown rice takes a bit longer to cook. I usually put it in a casserole in a 325°F oven for an hour or so. Wild rice is "spendy," as we say in Minnesota, and technically it is not rice, but a type of grass that takes longer to cook—up to an hour or longer. Your best guideline will be to read the directions on the package, as the rice processors will know the most about the specifics of their harvest.

Before we all had grills in our backyards and the grocery aisles were filled with hundreds of varieties of barbecue sauce, we had ketchup, mustard (the yellow kind), a few spices, granite-ware covered roaster pans and our ovens.

You could make this recipe in a slow cooker, but we think the ribs are better when each piece of meat stews in its own juices in a single layer.

Oven Barbecued Spareribs

SERVES 4 TO 6

2 to 3 pounds country-style pork ribs
1 to 3 teaspoons salt
½ teaspoon ground red pepper (cayenne)
vegetable oil for browning meat
2 small onions, very thinly sliced
2 tablespoons Worcestershire sauce
1 teaspoon paprika
¾ cup water
2 tablespoons vinegar
¾ cup catsup
1 teaspoon chili powder

Preheat oven to 350°F. Cut ribs into pieces. Season with salt and red pepper. Put a couple of tablespoons of vegetable oil into a frying pan and bring to medium heat. Add ribs and brown on all sides. Remove browned ribs and place in a single layer in a roasting pan with a cover (or in a large, deep baking pan covered with heavy aluminum foil). Cover ribs with sliced onions. Combine remaining ingredients and pour over ribs. Cover tightly and bake for 1½ to 2 hours, basting occasionally.

VARIATION: Soak ½ pound red or green lentils in 2 cups of water for 2 to 3 hours. Pare and cut 6 carrots into thick chunks. Put lentils and carrots in the bottom of the roaster and place other ingredients on top. Cook as above. Add more water as the lentils absorb the cooking juices.

RIB REFERENCE

Many backyard battles—if not wars—have been fought over the proper rib to serve. Beef or pork, meaty, traditional or baby-back, all have their fans. We prefer meaty country-style pork or beef short-ribs for this dish. They have more meat than the standard BBQ ribs and are better suited to long, slow cooking.

I remember the 1950s as school classrooms filled with 30 to 40 children; some didn't have desks at the beginning of the year. Summer days meant "going outside to play" all kinds of random games and diversions. Scores of us roamed the neighborhoods, in and out of our moms' kitchens, tearing across unfenced front yards and ducking through backyard gates. It was constant joyful chaos. Looking back, I wonder if the frequency Swiss steak was served had more to do with the opportunity for our mothers to vent on an innocent piece of meat—pounding in the flour while tenderizing with the pyramid-studded metal hammer—than with the fine-dining name. I don't think any of our fathers were fooled into thinking the flavorful main course had anything to do with a real "steak" dinner.

Swiss Steak

SERVES 4 TO 6

⅛ cup flour

1 teaspoon salt

½ teaspoon pepper

2 pounds round steak, cut 1½ to 2 inches thick

3 tablespoons vegetable oil or butter, or a mixture

1 small onion, sliced

1 (14- to 16-ounce) can tomatoes

Mix flour, salt and pepper. Pound into the surface of meat with a studded meat hammer. Heat oil over medium heat in a large frying pan that has a lid. Carefully place round steak in hot oil and cook on both sides until the meat is well browned. Remove meat to platter and add onion slices to the pan, cooking until they are translucent. Return meat and any accumulated juices to the frying pan and add tomatoes. Cover, lower the heat and simmer until meat is thoroughly cooked and tender, about 1½ hours. You may also wrap the meat, onion and tomatoes tightly in a heavy-duty aluminum foil package and roast in a 350°F oven for 1½ hours.

IOWA VARIATION

Use 1 can of undiluted condensed cream of mushroom soup instead of tomatoes.

MILWAUKEE VARIATION

Add to flour mixture:
> 1 tablespoon dry mustard

Add to tomatoes:
> ½ cup diced celery
> 1 tablespoon brown sugar
> 2 tablespoons Worcestershire sauce
> 1 tablespoon soy sauce

Stir in ¾ cup sour cream at end of cooking.

A messy kitchen is a happy kitchen and this kitchen is delirious.

UNKNOWN

Once upon a time there was a world without Ziploc bags or Tupperware containers. Leftovers were stored in lovely colored Pyrex containers with clear glass lids or wrapped up in "tin foil" or the less reliable waxed paper. Icebox freezing compartments, when they were completely defrosted, could hold a couple of ice cube trays, a pint of ice cream and two rectangular cardboard packages of frozen vegetables. Leftovers got used up almost immediately, converted into a tasty variation for dinner or fed to the family dog.

Inspired Beef Stroganoff

SERVES 4

2 cups leftover Sunday roast beef

1 (8-ounce) can sliced mushrooms

1 cup leftover gravy

½ cup sour cream

Combine all ingredients in a medium saucepan. Cook over low heat until warmed through and serve over noodles or leftover mashed potatoes.

The real Beef Stroganoff was a much fancier dish, certainly suitable for serving over beautiful egg noodles or rice to the Saturday evening card club.

Traditional Beef Stroganoff

SERVES 4 TO 6

1 pound beef tenderloin or
    top round sliced ¼-inch thick
    and cut into 3×2-inch pieces

¼ cup plus 2 tablespoons flour, divided

½ teaspoon salt

¼ teaspoon pepper

½ cup onion, chopped

1 small clove garlic, minced

½ pound mushrooms, sliced

¼ cup butter, melted in frying pan

¾ cup beef bouillon or beef stock

2 tablespoons sherry wine,
    not cooking wine

1 tablespoon tomato paste

2 tablespoons Worcestershire sauce

1 cup sour cream

¼ cup sliced green stuffed olives,
    optional

Dredge meat in ¼ cup flour seasoned with salt and pepper. Sauté onion, garlic and mushrooms in hot melted butter for several minutes. Add meat and brown on both sides. Remove meat and vegetables. Stir the 2 tablespoons flour into fat remaining in pan. Add beef bouillon slowly, then add wine, tomato paste and Worcestershire sauce. Cook, stirring, until thick. Add sour cream and heat slowly. Add beef and vegetables and optional sliced olives. Serve over noodles or rice.

I t must be a rule, if not a commandment. Lutheran church cookbooks must
have at least one recipe for Swedish meatballs. Deb and I expected to find
recipes for cream-sauce simmered pork and beef meatballs in the cookbooks
from Lutheran churches up and down the state and across the Midwest. But
we were astounded to find how far their influence had spread. Nearly every
church and community cookbook had at least one version of "Swedish" meatballs, even the Presbyterians and the Madison, Wisconsin, B'nai B'rith. We
found dozens of recipes we liked, and when these two were brought to the
taste-off, they were both winners. The Waverly Smorgasbord Meatballs (see
chapter 8) are also crowd pleasers.

Basic Meatball Method. The method for these meatballs is essentially
the same. Mix the ingredients in the order shown. Combine any liquid ingredients first before mixing into the meats. Form balls a bit larger than golf balls.
You can brown them in a frying pan, but I prefer to bake them in a preheated
350°F oven for 20 to 30 minutes (to an internal temperature of 160°F) and
then simmer them in a sauce if called for in the recipe.

Tried and True Swedish Meatballs

SERVES 6 TO 8

MEATBALLS

1 egg, lightly beaten

½ cup milk

2 tablespoons melted butter

1 cup fresh bread crumbs

1 pound ground beef

¼ pound lean ground pork

1½ teaspoons salt

2 teaspoons sugar

½ teaspoon allspice

¼ teaspoon nutmeg

GRAVY

3 tablespoons flour

1 teaspoon salt

⅛ teaspoon pepper

1½ cups water

½ cup cream

Preheat oven to 350°F. Make the meatballs following Basic Meatball Method above. When the meatballs are browned, put them in a casserole dish. Combine the gravy ingredients, mixing with a whisk so that there are no flour lumps. Pour over meatballs, cover and bake for 30 minutes.

Resorters' Meatballs

SERVES 12

MEATBALLS

2 pounds ground beef

1 pound lean ground pork

2 eggs

1 cup mashed potatoes

1 cup dry bread crumbs

1 teaspoon brown sugar

1½ teaspoons salt

½ teaspoon ginger

½ teaspoon cloves

½ teaspoon black pepper

½ teaspoon nutmeg

½ teaspoon allspice

1 cup milk

2 cups light cream

Mix all ingredients except cream and brown according to Basic Meatball Method above. Place in a casserole dish and pour cream over meatballs. Bake until warmed through, about 15 minutes.

Sunday evening was casual supper at our house. During the week we were not allowed to watch television during dinner. It was in the living room anyway. You could kind of see it from the dining room table if you looked through the archway and over the sofa. But on Sundays we brought out the TV trays and set them up in the living room. Dinner was accompanied by a side dish of history with our Sloppy Joes. As we settled in to sandwiches, chips and pickles, Walter Cronkite would assure us as we traveled back in time with CBS News historic re-creations that "everything you see here was as it happened that day, except . . . You Are There." In a 2003 interview on National Public Radio, Cronkite remarked that writers of many episodes were victims of the McCarthy-era blacklist and wrote using pen names. They used the tales of Joan of Arc, Galileo, and other figures to make thinly disguised points about contemporary witch hunts.

Sloppy Joes traveled through midwestern communities under disguises as well. Names and ingredients varied, but they all began with ground beef and ended up on a bun—with a lot of napkins at the ready.

Master Method for all recipes: Crumble the ground beef into a hot frying pan, add onion and cook until meat is brown and onion is transparent. Drain off fat and add remaining ingredients. Lower heat and simmer for a half hour or so and serve on buns.

A few recipes used fancy ingredients such as soy sauce or premade chili or barbeque sauce. Many of the recipes, like this one, featured condensed tomato soup.

Tavern Burgers

SERVES 6

1 pound hamburger	1 teaspoon sugar
1 large onion, minced	1 tablespoon vinegar
½ cup celery, chopped fine	3 tablespoons catsup
⅔ can condensed tomato soup	1 teaspoon dry mustard

Simple Joes

SERVES 4

1 pound ground beef
1 tablespoon Worcestershire sauce
few drops Tabasco
⅓ cup catsup

Sloppy Joes

SERVES 8

2 pounds hamburger
4 small onions, minced
1 tablespoon salt
few drops Tabasco
4 tablespoons mustard
1½ cups catsup
½ teaspoon chili powder

SERVING A CROWD

One church recipe for Society Hamburger is as far away from sloppy Tavern Burgers as you can get. The recipe said it "serves 35" from 3½ pounds of ground beef, 1 pound of onions, a bunch of celery, and 3 cups of tomato sauce. That works out to a little more than ¼ cup meat mixture per bun, so skimpy it sounds downright neat and tidy.

haven't made these dishes for years. They were mainstays back in the days of graduate school and toddlers about the house. Quick to put together, supper was on the table without having to pay attention and inexpensive, depending on the kind of chicken pieces used. The recipes could even rise to near elegance with the optional additions. Maybe they don't deserve to be at the back of the chapter. Instead, let's think of them as the Grand Finale. These two dishes will be easy to find when you want them in a hurry.

Chicken Tremendous

SERVES 6 TO 8

1 cup dry rice

1 envelope dry onion soup mix

1½ to 2 pounds chicken pieces or skinless, boneless chicken breasts

1 can condensed cream of chicken soup

1½ cups water or milk

Preheat oven to 350°F. Select a baking dish big enough to hold chicken pieces in one layer, deep enough to hold the liquids without spilling and suitable to serve from at the table. Lightly grease the dish. Put rice on the bottom and sprinkle dry soup mix over it. Lay the chicken pieces, skin side up, on top of rice. Mix chicken soup with water or milk and pour over chicken, lifting pieces so the liquid can flow under them. Cover with aluminum foil and bake until the rice is fluffy, about 45 minutes. Then remove foil and bake another 10 minutes until the chicken is cooked and browned.

Tuna Noodle Hot Dish

SERVES 4 TO 6

1 (8-ounce) package medium egg noodles

1 (6-ounce) can tuna

1 medium onion, diced

¼ cup diced green pepper

1 small jar red pimiento

4 to 6 ribs of celery, diced fine

1 can condensed cream of mushroom soup

paprika

1 cup crushed potato chips

OPTIONAL ADDITIONS

1 cup green peas

1 (7-ounce) can mushrooms, drained

Preheat oven to 350°F. Cook noodles until done in boiling water; drain. Drain tuna and add to noodles along with vegetables and soup. Mix well and spoon into a buttered 2-quart casserole dish. Sprinkle generously with paprika and crushed potato chips. Bake about an hour until heated through and bubbly.

VEGETABLES

Rae Katherine Eighmey

I suspect the best food we know is the remembered food of our childhood. . . . Along our fencerows in May wild asparagus spears skyward, and at the edges of our southern woodlands after spring's first warm rain wait the pyramidal, honeycombed miracles of morels. . . . The flavors and fragrances of Wisconsin's kitchens are myriad and wonderful, the sweet corn rushed from field to pot to table. . . . These are joys to cherish in a teetering age of hydrogen bombs and packaged mixes and it is heartwarming to find them remembered and recorded here.

EDWARD HARRIS HETH, BE *MILWAUKEE'S GUEST*,
JUNIOR LEAGUE OF MILWAUKEE

The women of the Waverly Lutheran Church near Truman, Minnesota, really loved their vegetables. Their 1954 cookbook featured 47 pages of vegetables and salads with recipes "worthy of the most careful concern you would lavish on a cake or an elegant dessert." Promoting increased enjoyment of this food group took on nearly missionary status as "a survey of diets . . . revealed that less than half of the adults and less than one-third of the children were eating satisfactory amounts of the green and yellow vegetables."

Mrs. James Peterson provided "a special recipe of preparing cabbage by my mother Mrs. August Mau."

Sweet and Sour Cabbage

SERVES 8

1 medium-sized head red cabbage, finely shredded

2 medium onions, chopped fine

1 apple, peeled, cored and diced

2 strips bacon, diced

2 cups water

2 tablespoons vinegar

2 tablespoons brown sugar

½ teaspoon salt

2 tablespoons caraway seeds

¼ teaspoon pepper

2 tablespoons butter

Prepare cabbage, onion and apple as described in the ingredient list. In a large frying pan with a lid, fry bacon over medium heat until crisp. Remove bacon bits and set aside. Add the shredded cabbage and sauté in bacon fat about 5 minutes. Add onion and apple. Pour in water, cover and reduce heat to low. Cook for about 20 minutes or until vegetables are tender. Add vinegar, brown sugar, salt, caraway seeds, pepper and butter. Cover and cook for another 20 minutes over very low heat. Remove to serving platter and sprinkle with reserved crispy bacon bits.

CONQUERING CABBAGE

You need a large sharp knife to manage cabbage for this delightful dish. First remove any loose tough outer leaves and rinse off the outside of the cabbage. Make a thin slice across the stem end to provide a firmer base. Balancing the head on the stem end, carefully cut it in half. Then cut out the center by slicing a "V" into the center to remove the tough solid core. Turn the head over onto the flat side and slice into thin slices working from top to bottom.

Some cookbook committees sought recipes from the very best cooks in the community even if they weren't members of the congregation or group. The editors of the Waverly Lutheran cookbook got this delicious parsnip preparation from "guest cook" Edwina Hammerand.

Parsnip Ring

SERVES 6 TO 8

1 pound parsnips, peeled, chopped and boiled
   for 10 to 15 minutes, until very tender
1 tablespoon onion juice
2 tablespoons butter
1 tablespoon flour
1 teaspoon salt
3 eggs, separated

Preheat oven to 350°F. Mash cooked parsnips. You should have about 1⅓ cups. Add onion juice, butter, flour and salt. Mix well. Lightly beat the egg yolks and add them to parsnips. Whip the egg whites until stiff. Fold them into the parsnip mixture. Pour the mixture into a well-greased 5-cup ring mold (see page 135 for tips). Place ring mold in a pan and pour hot water around it so the water comes halfway up the side of the mold. Bake until firm in the center, about 45 minutes.

Just about every vegetable recipe in the cookbooks we looked at involved enrobing the nutrient-rich peas, carrots, green beans, or potatoes with rich white sauce. We've all eaten our share and then some. Vegetables, white sauce, and potlucks go together in the Midwest. Certainly such dishes are delicious, but sometimes cookbooks brought forth vegetable preparations without a speck of cream. This tasty and easy carrot dish would be a hit at any potluck.

Minted Carrots

SERVES 4

1 pound carrots, thinly sliced
4 tablespoons butter
2 tablespoons mint jelly

Cook carrots until tender. Melt butter and add jelly, stirring until jelly is melted and the two are blended together. Pour over carrots just before serving.

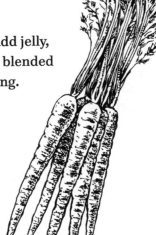

I love beets, but I don't like waiting for them to cook. This preparation reduces the cooking time to 15 minutes or so. The touch of nutmeg is a subtle accent. This will be a family favorite. Only problem with beets: peeling and slicing them. Peeled beets can stain. So take care where you put them, and wash your hands right away.

Basic Beets

SERVES 4

3 large whole fresh beets
2 tablespoons butter
1 teaspoon sugar
pinch salt
dash black pepper
⅛ teaspoon nutmeg
1 or 2 large lettuce leaves, remove before serving

Peel raw beets and slice paper thin with a food processor or vegetable slicer. Melt butter in saucepan. Add sugar, salt, pepper and nutmeg. Add the sliced beets and stir to coat well with butter mixture. Rinse the lettuce leaves in cold water, shake some of the water off and place them on top of the beets. Turn heat down to very low, cover pot and let the beets steam until done, about 15 minutes.

My picky friend Emma loved fresh green beans, but she would serve only the tiniest baby ones. When gardening friends brought by baskets of fully ripe beans, she would raise her critical eyebrow after they left and toss the beans into the Saturday morning pot of "leftover soup." Had Emma known of this sauce, those mature pods would have starred on the prime time dinner table. The Herb Sauce can be frozen in cubes and tossed with beans, peas, asparagus or any green vegetable.

Green Beans in Herb Sauce

SERVES 4

¼ pound butter (1 stick)

¾ cup minced onion

1 minced clove garlic

¼ cup minced celery

¼ teaspoon dried basil

¼ cup snipped parsley

¼ teaspoon dried rosemary

¾ teaspoon salt

1 pound fresh green beans, cooked

Melt butter in a medium saucepan. Add onion, garlic and celery. Cook over low heat for about 5 minutes until the onion and celery are tender. Add basil, parsley, rosemary and salt. Cover and simmer for 10 minutes. Toss well with drained beans.

German Potato Salad stuffed in a potato. Great idea. Even better flavor. This delicious recipe serves eight. We liked it so much that we discovered the topping will keep in the refrigerator or freezer so you can make it even if you want to serve two, or even just one.

Hot Baked Potato Salad

YIELD: 1 POTATO PER PERSON

8 washed baking potatoes
vegetable oil
8 strips bacon, fried, reserving ⅔ cup drippings
½ cup minced onion
½ cup minced green pepper
1 teaspoon salt
¼ teaspoon black pepper
4 teaspoons sugar
6 tablespoons vinegar

About an hour and 15 minutes before serving, rub potatoes with vegetable oil and bake until done. Cook the bacon until crisp. Crumble bacon and set aside. Add onion and green pepper and cook until onion is transparent. Add salt, black pepper and sugar. When potatoes are done, cut in half and scoop out insides into a bowl. Add vinegar and mash. Combine with bacon mixture and restuff potato skins.

SINGLE SERVING AND HEART HEALTHY-ISH ADAPTATION

I really like this baked potato salad recipe, but I don't need to cook 8 potatoes every time I want to eat it. With family cholesterol numbers in the stratosphere I don't need to serve bacon fat either. This adaptation solves both problems. Bake a potato whenever you want and mix with dressing stored in refrigerator or freezer. Make enough dressing for 8 potatoes following this method: Cook bacon on paper towels in the microwave to capture and discard the fat. Heat ¼ cup vegetable oil in a frying pan over low heat. Flavor the oil by simmering the cooked bacon in it for a few minutes. Remove bacon, add onion and green pepper and sauté until onion is transparent. While this is cooking, combine salt, black pepper, sugar and vinegar. Add vinegar mixture to vegetables. Cut potato in half and open it up by cutting cross hatches through it. Spoon 1 to 2 tablespoons of the dressing over potato and sprinkle bacon bits on top. Refrigerate leftover dressing and reheat before using. ADDITIONAL NOTE: Vegetarians or those who don't eat pork could flavor the oil with nonmeat "bacon" products.

Even in the meat-and-potatoes 1950s, vegetables stepped up and served as main dishes. This carrot loaf is filling and well flavored. The vegetable curry is a satisfying main dish with a subtle blend of spices.

Carrot Loaf

SERVES 8

2 pounds carrots, scraped, chopped and cooked until very tender

¾ cup minced celery

½ cup finely chopped onion

2 tablespoons butter

¾ cup cracker crumbs or dry bread crumbs

3 eggs, lightly beaten

1 teaspoon salt

⅛ teaspoon pepper

½ teaspoon dried savory, crushed

Preheat oven to 350°F. Mash the carrots and measure out 4 cups. Sauté celery and onion in butter. Combine carrots with crumbs, eggs and seasonings. Add celery and onions. Line bottom of greased loaf pan with foil. Spread in mixture. Bake until firm, about 35 minutes.

Mixed Vegetable Curry

SERVES 4 AS A MAIN COURSE

4 to 6 cups fresh vegetables—a mixture of celery, eggplant,
    peas, green beans, potatoes, cauliflower and tomatoes

¼ cup butter, sesame oil or peanut oil

½ teaspoon cumin seed

½ cup lukewarm water

salt to taste

⅛ teaspoon red (cayenne) pepper

⅛ teaspoon turmeric

⅛ teaspoon coriander

¼ teaspoon curry powder

Peel eggplant; the other vegetables can remain unpeeled. Wash, trim and cut
vegetables into large pieces (about 1 inch). Heat butter or oil in a large frying
pan that has a lid. Add cumin seed and stir until it becomes lightly toasted.
Add vegetables and water, stir quickly and cover. Lower the heat and simmer
until vegetables are crisp tender, about 5 to 10 minutes, depending on size of
vegetables and pan. Combine remaining spices and sprinkle over the vegetables. Stir gently and cook for 3 or 4 more minutes. Serve over rice.

orn *is* the Midwest. Drive on any interstate highway from March through October and you'll see it growing in Grant Wood patterns, forming the economic tapestry of small-town survival. From July through September, back roads, side streets, and shopping malls are decorated with farmers' pickup trucks, their beds overflowing with golden goodness. Nearly 700,000 acres of sweet corn are harvested every year. In the 1950s, however, sweet-corn varieties were not as sweet. For the best flavor, if you didn't have the pot boiling before you picked the corn from the garden, it seemed hardly worth the effort. These two recipes use canned corn from the bumper crops picked and packed in Minnesota and Wisconsin to capture the flavor of summer.

Corn and Tomato Casserole

SERVES 6 TO 8

2 (14- to 16-ounce) cans whole kernel corn, drained,
   or 12 ears fresh corn, kernels removed
2 (14- to 16-ounce) cans diced tomatoes
1 cup fine cracker crumbs or dry bread crumbs
salt and pepper
2 tablespoons butter

Preheat oven to 350°F. Lightly grease a 2-quart casserole dish. Layer ingredients as follows: 1 cup of the corn, 1 cup of the tomatoes, ¼ cup of the crumbs; repeat. Season with salt and pepper to taste. Dot the top with butter. Cover and bake for 20 minutes. Uncover and bake for 10 minutes longer. If the casserole is too dry, add a small amount of tomato juice or water.

Corn Pudding

SERVES 6 TO 8

1 (14- to 16-ounce) can whole kernel corn, drained,
    or 6 ears fresh corn, kernels removed

2 eggs, well beaten

1 tablespoon soft butter

1 cup milk

¼ teaspoon salt

dash of pepper

Preheat oven to 350°F. Mix corn, eggs, butter and milk. Season with salt and pepper. Pour into greased 2-quart baking dish and set dish in a pan of hot water (see page 135 for tips). Bake until a knife inserted in the center comes out clean, about 50 to 60 minutes.

REMOVING KERNELS FROM FRESH CORN

In season, today's fresh corn is so tender you can substitute it for canned in these recipes. To harvest the kernels from the cobs, first remove the husks and silk. Hold an ear of corn upright in a large bowl. (Anchor your bowl so it won't slip by placing a damp dish towel under it.) Very carefully place a sturdy chef's knife at the top of the ear and slice down through the kernels. Once the kernels are removed, press the back edge of the knife firmly against the cob and run it down to the base, extracting the milk.

Potatoes are at the root of hearty midwestern meals. It is easy to think of sweet potatoes or yams as appearing on tables only at Thanksgiving and Christmas. We were pleasantly surprised to find a number of recipes that expanded or even contradicted the overly sweet typical sweet potatoes or yams-with-marshmallows casserole. The take on scalloped potatoes replaces white sauce with mayonnaise and the long baking time with a short broil. The caraway seeds lend an interesting zest to this fairly quick dish.

Scalloped Sweet Potatoes and Oranges

SERVES 4

2 medium-sized sweet potatoes, about 1½ pounds

2 large oranges, peeled and cut into sections, about 1½ cups

1 teaspoon grated orange rind

1 teaspoon salt

2 tablespoons sugar

2 tablespoons butter

½ cup orange juice

Preheat oven to 350°F. Peel sweet potatoes and cut into ¼-inch circular slices. Lightly grease a 2-quart casserole. Put a layer of sweet potato slices in the bottom of the dish, then a layer of orange sections. Sprinkle with grated orange rind, salt and sugar and dot with butter. Repeat until all ingredients are used. Pour orange juice over top and cover. Bake 45 minutes to 1 hour.

Waldorf Sweet Potato Salad

SERVES 4

2 cups sweet potatoes cooked,
    peeled and cut in ½-inch cubes

1 cup sliced celery

1 cup cored and chopped apple

½ cup chopped walnuts

2 tablespoons lemon juice

½ teaspoon salt

2 teaspoons sugar

½ cup or more mayonnaise

Mix sweet potatoes, celery, apple and walnuts in a large bowl. Squeeze lemon juice over the ingredients. Sprinkle with salt and sugar. Stir in mayonnaise to taste. Chill for at least a half hour before serving.

Bubbly Broiled Potatoes

SERVES 4

4 medium white potatoes

3 tablespoons mayonnaise

4 tablespoons grated cheese

1 teaspoon caraway seed or more

Boil unpeeled potatoes until tender. Cool slightly, peel and cut in ⅓-inch-thick slices. Arrange slices in a square baking pan suitable for serving at the table. Spread mayonnaise over potatoes; sprinkle with cheese and caraway seed. Place under the broiler, about 5 to 6 inches away from flame, with broiler on low heat. Cook until potatoes are golden, about 5 minutes.

5

INTERNATIONAL and HERITAGE RECIPES

Debbie Miller

Imagine a long, beautifully decorated table, laden with foods—some familiar and some not to many midwestern cooks in the 1950s. I worked as a waitress in a lovely old fjord hotel in Norway, and the luncheon cold table (with warm dishes) always wowed the guests entering the dining room. Carefully arranged on blue and white Royal Copenhagen dishes on a snowy white tablecloth were platters of sliced meats, an enormous whole salmon (sans skin and bones), an array of salads, several kinds of herring, a rosemaled basket of breads and rolls, pastel desserts piped with whipped cream and a huge yellow sheetcake covered with whipped cream and decorated with fresh fruit. On a hot tray on one corner were the warm dishes, traditional fish cakes and cream porridge.

Our midwestern smorgasbord draws on an array of dishes from the ethnic heritages of the region's settlers, combined with an assortment of contemporary international dishes and sophisticated foods that appeared in a select few 1950s community cookbooks. Two in the Minnesota Historical Society's collection are the University of Minnesota's *Curriculum for Cooks*, published by the faculty women's club and hospitals auxiliary, and the Alexandria Golf Club's *Par Recipes* (3rd edition), compiled by a creative combination of local women and regular visitors to area resorts from big cities in and beyond the Midwest—Chicago, Kansas City, and Dallas. Many church cookbooks of the era, like the *Noted Recipes* cookbook of the Swedish-heritage First Covenant Church of Duluth and the Norwegian Lutheran Memorial Church of Minneapolis's *Cook Book of Tested Recipes* (2nd edition), included old-country recipes. Other books, like one from St. Mary of Mount Carmel in Long Prairie, Minnesota, gave a vivid sense of ethnic history not with their recipes but by telling colorful tales of church founding.

In the late afternoon of October 12, 1867, when Fr. Buh [a Slovenian priest who founded many Roman Catholic congregations in central and northern Minnesota] came trudging into Long Prairie over the hills from Little Falls with his Mass kit swung from a stick over his shoulder, it was a kind pioneer mother who welcomed him to her home with a hearty meal. The Vennewitz home became his church and lodging. We can well imagine the aroma of coffee, bacon and eggs and Mother Vennewitz's favorite coffee cake [unfortunately not preserved in this collection] after Mass in the morning when [all] gathered around the kitchen table.

—*St Mary's Cook Book*

These cookbooks also provide a unique perspective on the Upper Midwest's international connections in the era, some built on the ties of immigrants and their descendants and others on the land-grant universities' and other colleges' ability to attract students and faculty from all over the world.

Recipes from Iran, Uganda, Jordan, India, Japan and Czechoslovakia were notable in the St. Paul YWCA World Fellowship Committee's *Y's Favorites* cookbook, which emphasized internationalism. Contributors included the first U.S. woman ambassador, Eugenie Anderson of Red Wing, and Ruth Armajani, the wife of a Macalester College professor from Iran, whose Persian Sweet Rice recipe is included here. Iranian-born Yahya Armajani was a favorite history professor at Macalester College in St. Paul during my time there in the 1960s. Dr. and Mrs. A. often invited students to their home for delicious dinners.

Shereen P' Sough (Persian Sweet Rice)

RUTH ARMAJANI

SERVES 12

¼ cup dates, chopped

5 to 6 medium-sized carrots, peeled and sliced

½ cup walnuts

½ cup pecans

½ cup almonds

1 cup raisins

2 teaspoons olive oil

3 quarts plus ⅓ cup water, divided

3 cups raw rice

3 tablespoons salt

¼ cup butter

Fry dates, carrots, nuts and raisins in olive oil in a nonstick skillet until lightly browned; set aside. Bring 3 quarts of the water to a boil in a 4- or 5-quart pot. Add rice and salt. Bring to a boil and cook 4 minutes, then drain into a large colander. Sprinkle rice with a little cold water to prevent sticking. Melt butter in the pot where you cooked the rice and add ⅓ cup of the water. Then return rice and carrot mixture to the pot in layers, beginning and ending with rice. Cover pot with a heavy, tight-fitting lid. Steam for 1 hour over a low flame on top of the stove. Taste rice from the top layer. If it's still crunchy, as it may be depending on what kind of rice you use, you may need to add another ¼ cup water after the hour is up. If so, cover the pot and steam another 15 minutes. Serve with chicken. (Mrs. Armajani specified fried chicken, but a rotisserie fowl from the grocery store would work well, as would leftover turkey.)

During our research for this book we found two Jewish cookbooks, one published by a women's group at a Minneapolis Reform temple, the other by B'nai B'rith Women in Madison, Wisconsin, that provided a wide array of heritage recipes from that religious tradition. The Women's League of Minneapolis's Beth El Synagogue compiled a book of recipes for Jewish holidays—the Sabbath, Sukkot, Hanukkah, Yom Kippur, Passover and others—introducing them with the idea that a vital ingredient in these religious festivals "can be yours with the skillful application of a woman's mighty weapon—'the cooking spoon.'"

When I was testing recipes early in September, the butcher at my never-fail meat market reported he couldn't afford the space for the beef bones this soup requires until late fall. He sold me a nice 1-pound pot roast with some fat on it and cut it into ½-inch cubes. At the supermarket I found frozen beef bones packed and labeled for pets, and I snapped them up, using one in this recipe. The other is in my freezer for the next batch of this lovely soup. It's too good to wait until winter to make it again.

Hanukkah Hearty Barley Soup

FROM *COOK FOR THE HOLIDAYS*, BETH EL SYNAGOGUE, MINNEAPOLIS

SERVES 8

½ pound beef
2 tablespoons vegetable oil or fat
2 pounds beef soup bones
2 tablespoons minced parsley
¼ teaspoon pepper
2 quarts water

¼ cup barley
1 cup chopped carrots
½ cup chopped onion
½ cup chopped celery
2 cups cooked tomatoes
1 cup fresh or frozen peas

Cut meat into cubes (or ask butcher to do it). Heat the oil or fat in a large soup pot. Add the beef cubes and brown on all sides. Add the bones, parsley, pepper and water. Cover tightly and cook on low heat for 1 hour. Add barley and cook 1 hour longer. Cool several hours in the refrigerator (or in Minnesota, on the back porch at Hanukkah time) or overnight. Skim off excess fat that comes to the top and solidifies. Remove soup bone. Add chopped vegetables except peas. Bring to simmer and cook 45 minutes. Add peas and continue cooking 15 minutes if using fresh peas or 5 minutes for frozen.

Not all the postwar community cookbooks contained down-home recipes for good, plain Upper Midwest-style cooking. Sometimes "down home" was an African American food tradition from the American South that would have looked exotic to European American meat-and-potatoes eaters. Historic Pilgrim Baptist Church's *A Book of Favorite Recipes* featured delectable dishes like the Shrimp Creole and Sweet Potato Pie included here.

Shrimp Creole

NILEE LEWIS

SERVES 4

¼ cup butter

1 large onion, chopped

½ cup chopped green pepper

1 tablespoon salt, or less to taste

dash of pepper

⅛ teaspoon paprika

2 cups cooked or canned tomatoes

¼ teaspoon Tabasco sauce, more if desired

1⅓ cup cleaned, cooked shrimp

2 to 3 cups cooked rice as an accompaniment

Melt butter in a large frying pan over medium heat. Watch carefully as butter will start to burn quickly. Add onion and green pepper. Cook, stirring from time to time until the pepper is tender and the onion is transparent. Add salt, pepper, paprika and tomatoes. Bring to a boil, add Tabasco sauce, then lower heat and simmer for 10 minutes. Stir in the shrimp and heat through. Serve over hot rice.

Sweet Potato Pie

CORINNE DICKERSON, CLARKSVILLE, TENNESSEE

YIELD: 1 PIE, SERVING 8 TO12

4 cups hot mashed sweet potatoes

½ cup (1 stick) butter

1 cup white sugar

½ teaspoon nutmeg

1 teaspoon vanilla

3 eggs, well beaten

1 unbaked 9-inch pie shell

Preheat oven to 400°F. Put hot mashed sweet potatoes into a large bowl. Add butter and mix well until butter is melted and thoroughly incorporated. Stir in sugar, nutmeg, vanilla and the well-beaten eggs. Mix well and pour into the unbaked pie shell. Bake at 400°F for 10 minutes; reduce heat to 350°F and bake another 30 to 35 minutes or until a knife inserted in the center comes out clean.

HOW TO GET 4 CUPS MASHED SWEET POTATOES

Bake 4 medium sweet potatoes until very soft. Carefully peel and cut out any bad spots. Or use 2 (16- to 18-ounce) cans of sweet potatoes, drained and heated until very hot—this will give you more than enough. Mash hot baked or canned potatoes with a potato masher or whip with an electric mixer until free of lumps. The goal is a perfectly smooth mash. To measure, pack potatoes firmly into measuring cup and level off top.

The population of a state with a deserved reputation for being mostly white and northern European became a bit more diverse during and after World War II, as Japanese Americans moved to Minnesota from the internment camps of the West. Several of these new Minnesotans contributed recipes to the Pilgrim Baptist cookbook at the request of African American co-workers who were church members, so that recipes for Beef Sukiyaki and Eggs Fu Yung sat alongside those for Fried Green Tomatoes and Southern Fried Oysters. Pilgrim churchwomen also asked Mexican American friends and co-workers to contribute recipes, making Pilgrim's cookbook the only 1950s compilation we found that included recipes for Tamales, Tacos, and even Tortillas, all contributed by women members of a group that had been settling in St. Paul since the 1920s.

Beef Sukiyaki

HATSUME AKAKI

SERVES 4

NOTE: The original recipe called for rendered beef suet instead of oil and for a teaspoon of "gourmet powder" which we took to be MSG. To our taste there is plenty of salt and flavor in the soy sauce, sugar and vegetables.

2 medium-to-large onions, peeled, halved and sliced thin

1 green pepper, halved and sliced thin

1 bunch green onions, roots trimmed and cut in 1½-inch lengths using both green and white parts

1 pound lean tender beef such as sirloin, filet or tenderloin

¼ (6–8 ounce) package bean thread noodles

2 tablespoons vegetable oil

3 tablespoons sugar

⅓ cup soy sauce, low-sodium if preferred

1 (8-ounce) can sliced bamboo shoots

Boiled rice as an accompaniment, about ½ cup cooked rice per person

Prepare the vegetables as listed in the ingredients and set aside. Slice beef into 2×1-inch pieces. Put the noodles in a heatproof bowl, pour in enough boiling water to cover them completely, stir and set aside to soften. Heat oil in large frying pan with a lid over medium heat. Carefully add the beef pieces, stir and cook until the pink is almost gone. While the meat is cooking, combine the sugar and soy sauce, stirring until sugar is dissolved. Pour half of this mixture over beef; add drained bamboo shoots, sliced onions and green pepper. Mix well, cover and cook over medium heat about 8 minutes, until vegetables are tender, but still crisp. While mixture is cooking, drain the bean thread noodles and snip into pieces about 1½ inches long. Add noodles, green onions and the remaining soy sauce mixture. Cover and cook about 3 more minutes until onions begin to wilt and everything is heated through.

More international recipes found their way into the Minneapolis Symphony's *Encore*, proudly subtitled "A Cookbook of the Favorite Dishes of the World's Most Famous Musicians," with lively illustrations provided by Maestro Antal Dorati. Some recipes used familiar ingredients differently or added unaccustomed seasonings like garlic and olive oil. Other recipes combined exotic ingredients rarely seen in 1950s church cookbooks.

Filovane Paprika (Stuffed Peppers à la Yugoslav)

NORMAN SCOTT

SERVES 4 TO 6

green bell peppers, 6 small or 4 large

2 tablespoons olive oil

1 small onion, diced

1 pound ground veal

1 pound lean ground beef

½ cup rice, uncooked

½ teaspoon salt

¼ teaspoon pepper

¼ teaspoon paprika

1 egg, lightly beaten

2 tablespoons water

1 to 2 tablespoons sugar

1 (14- to 16-ounce) can tomato sauce

Preheat oven to 350°F. Carefully slice tops off peppers, about ¼-inch down from the stem. Clean out the seeds, ribs and membranes and set aside. Put the oil in a frying pan over medium heat. Add onion and cook, stirring frequently, until it becomes transparent. Cool slightly. Gently combine veal, beef, rice, salt, pepper, paprika, egg, water and cooked onions. Stuff the peppers with the mixture and place them in a baking dish. Put the tops back on the peppers. Combine sugar with tomato sauce and pour this mixture around the peppers. Bake until peppers are tender and the meat and rice are cooked to an internal temperature of 160°F, about 1 hour.

Pomodori al riso (Tomatoes Stuffed with Rice)

FERNANDO PREVITALI

SERVES 4 AS A SIDE DISH

2 very large tomatoes

1 tablespoon uncooked rice

¼ teaspoon salt

1½ tablespoons chopped fresh parsley

1 to 2 cloves garlic, minced

1 tablespoon olive oil

Preheat oven to 350°F. Slice the tomatoes in two, leaving about ⅔ of the tomato on the bottom. With a large spoon, gently remove the pulp, juice and seeds; mix with rice. Add salt, parsley and garlic. Stuff mixture into the bottoms, mounding to fit. Put a little oil in a baking dish and place the tomatoes on it. Put tops back on and drizzle with olive oil. Bake until rice is done, about 1½ hours. Cut in half to serve.

Salad Tropicale

MASSIMO FRECCIA

SERVES 6

1 fresh pineapple

2 large ripe avocados

DRESSING

6 tablespoons oil

2 tablespoons vinegar

½ teaspoon salt

Cut pineapple in half the long way. Cut out the core. Scoop out fruit, keeping skins whole, and cut fruit into small squares. Peel avocados and cut into small squares. Add to pineapple pieces. Whisk oil, vinegar, and salt in a small bowl until emulsified (oil no longer separates from vinegar). Dress the salad. Stuff pineapple halves with the salad and serve.

This recipe is adapted for lighter tastes and better health. The original recipe, contributed by Mrs. Arnold Ley to the cookbook *Our Heavenly Recipes,* by the Ladies of St. Mary's Congregation, Menomonee Falls, Wisconsin, called for equal amounts of potatoes and bacon. You're welcome to give that a try, but even my bacon-loving husband thought this version of the recipe had plenty of it. The recipe works best with a good meaty bacon, so, as the original author suggested, buy "the best quality you can afford."

Good Old German Potato Salad

8 TO 12 SERVINGS

3 pounds small new red potatoes, well scrubbed

1 pound bacon, diced

1 teaspoon salt

¼ to ½ teaspoon black pepper

1 large onion, minced

1½ cups chopped celery

chopped radishes, parsley (or tender dandelion greens, in season), hard-cooked eggs, optional

DRESSING:

2 tablespoons butter

1 tablespoon flour

1 teaspoon sugar

2 tablespoons bacon fat (reserved)

½ cup cider vinegar

½ cup water

Cook the potatoes in boiling water until a sharp knife point can just pierce them easily. While potatoes are cooking, fry the bacon in a large frying pan. (You may want to do this in two batches so that the bacon crisps well.) Drain bacon on paper towels and pour off all but 2 tablespoons of the fat and set aside until the potatoes are done. Drain cooked potatoes and slice each into four or five pieces. (If you prefer them without the peel, remove it before slicing.) Season with salt and pepper and add minced onion, chopped celery, fried bacon pieces and any of the optional ingredients. Mix together gently.

To make the dressing, add butter, flour and sugar to reserved bacon fat in the frying pan. Blend well with whisk or wooden spoon. Add the vinegar and water. Bring to a boil over medium heat, lower heat and let dressing bubble slowly, stirring from time to time as it thickens, for about 3 or 4 minutes. Pour dressing over hot potatoes. Again, mix gently. Serve hot or warm.

This tasty dish appeared in the cookbook of the Hospital Service League of Sycamore, Illinois. It's nice because you don't have to fry the meatballs. They bake in the oven in beef stock.

Köenigsberger Klops (German Meatballs)

VIRGINIA N. OVITZ

SERVES 6 TO 8

NOTE: Like many meatball recipes from this era, this recipe uses three meats: beef, pork and veal. In tests we found that substituting more beef for the veal didn't make much difference in the end product. We also used at least 90 percent lean ground beef. If you don't have ground pork available at your market, you can purchase a half pound of pork and process it in a food processor to approximate ground pork. I used the full-strength beef stock that comes in waxed boxes and in cans. If you are using condensed beef broth, dilute it according to instructions on container and use 2 cups of the diluted broth.

½ pound each ground beef, pork and veal (see Note)

2 slices white bread soaked in water, squeezed out
    and broken into small pieces

2 eggs, well beaten

¼ cup finely minced onion

3 tablespoons minced fresh parsley

1 teaspoon salt or less if you prefer

¼ teaspoon paprika

1 teaspoon lemon juice

1 teaspoon Worcestershire sauce

2 cups (16 ounces) beef stock or consommé,
    lower-sodium version (see Note)

2 cups water

GRAVY:

2 tablespoons butter

2 tablespoons flour

2 tablespoons finely chopped dill pickles

juice of half a lemon

1–2 cups reserved beef juices

Preheat oven to 350°F. Combine meat, bread, eggs, onion, parsley, salt and paprika. Mix well and shape lightly into 2-inch balls. Place in large casserole or 13×9-inch glass pan. Combine lemon juice and Worcestershire sauce with beef stock and water; pour over meatballs to almost cover. Bake uncovered for 45 minutes (to an internal temperature of 160°F). Remove meatballs and keep warm. Reserve beef juices to make gravy. Melt butter in small 2-quart saucepan over medium heat. Sprinkle flour over butter and stir, cooking for several minutes until mixture is bubbly. Then add pickles and lemon juice and stir thoroughly. Add in the pan juices gradually, stirring with a whisk to prevent lumps as the gravy thickens. (You may not need all the pan juices.) Pour over meatballs and serve.

ike the Minneapolis Symphony, the St. Louis Symphony's Women's Association produced a cookbook with many sophisticated recipes in the 1950s, including Mexico City Tamale Pie. The recipe donor wrote that the original of the dish was served at "the famous Sanborn's restaurant in Mexico City." The cheese and green chile tamales I bought at St. Paul's El Burrito Mercado were perfect for the following dish, giving it some heat but not too much. Chicken tamales would also be good.

Mexico City Tamale Pie

MRS. P. J. NEFF

SERVES 4 TO 6

6 tamales
1 cooked bone-in chicken breast or 2 boneless breasts
¾ cup grated Parmesan cheese

SAUCE:
1 cup canned tomato sauce
½ cup chili sauce or salsa
1 cup whole kernel corn
1 to 2 tablespoons granulated sugar
2 tablespoons vegetable oil
½ cup seedless raisins
10 ripe olives cut in strips
salt and pepper

Unwrap tamales and split lengthwise. Slice or break chicken breast into small bite-sized pieces. Place split tamales in greased baking dish and lay chicken pieces over them. Mix sauce ingredients and pour over chicken and tamales. Sprinkle with Parmesan cheese. Bake at 375°F for 45 minutes. Good served with garlic bread and guacamole.

An English couple exchanged homes with the Rev. and Mrs. Charles Nelson of Worthington. At a picnic in honor of the visitors arranged by the First Methodist congregation, there was discussion about the word "potluck," which was a new term for the Britishers. "At home we call it a 'faith meal,'" the English lady smiled, explaining, "We must have faith that there will be enough food for everyone." My recollection of potlucks attended on this side of the pond is that there's rarely a problem with enough food; where faith is required is that there'll be a good mix of main dishes, salads, and desserts.

DORTHY RICKERS COOKBOOK: MIXING AND MUSING, WORTHINGTON, MN (1983)

Pizza pies reportedly piggybacked to the United States with soldiers who served in Italy during World War II. Some cities had pizzerias before the war, but in the Midwest, the pizza restaurant, not to mention home delivery, was yet to take over neighborhoods. We saw all kinds of "pizza" recipes. Many were miniature pizzas to be served as a cocktail snack rather than as a main course and used incongruous ingredients: English muffins, even the small slices of party rye bread as a base with American cheese, unseasoned tomato sauce and perhaps olives as a topping.

We found some Italian-influenced dishes in big-city cookbooks. The St. Louis Symphony book featured dueling antipasto plates with complex marinated vegetables next to rolled anchovies and salami. But we were surprised to find a real yeast-dough, anchovy-topped pizza in the Kappa Kappa Kappa cookbook from Greenfield, Indiana.

Pizza Pie

SERVES 4

DOUGH:
1 package dry yeast
2 tablespoons lukewarm water
1 cup boiling water
2 tablespoons shortening
1½ teaspoons salt
3 cups all purpose flour

Sprinkle yeast on top of the 2 tablespoons warm water; let stand until dissolved and beginning to foam. Pour 1 cup boiling water over shortening and salt in a large bowl. Cool to lukewarm and stir in yeast. Add half of the flour and beat until smooth. Add the remaining flour and knead into a smooth dough.

Divide dough in half for two 11-inch thin-crust pizzas, or use the complete recipe for one 13-inch thick-crust pizza. Form dough into rounds and place on greased cookie sheets. Make edges thicker to keep toppings from escaping during baking. Let rise in warm place until doubled.

TOMATO TOPPING:

3 tablespoons olive oil

½ cup Parmesan cheese

¾ pound sliced mozzarella cheese

2 cups ripe tomatoes, diced, or
    1 (14- to 16-ounce) can diced tomatoes, drained

1 minced clove garlic

½ teaspoon salt

½ teaspoon pepper

½ teaspoon dried oregano

½ teaspoon dried thyme

Preheat oven to 450°F. Brush dough with 1 tablespoon of the olive oil and sprinkle with Parmesan cheese, then arrange half the mozzarella on top. Combine tomatoes with garlic, salt and pepper; sprinkle on top, followed by remaining cheese. Sprinkle with dried herbs and drizzle with remaining 2 tablespoons of the olive oil. Bake until crust is golden brown, 20 to 30 minutes.

VARIATIONS:

Pepperoni Pizza: Add pepperoni slices on top of tomatoes.

Anchovy Pizza: Make pizza as directed for tomato topping, except omit all oil and cheese. Dot tomatoes with 2 ounces of fillet anchovies, finely minced, and strips of green peppers. Drizzle with oil from anchovy can. Bake as directed.

Seasoned consumers of Pepparkakor let us know that this recipe produced a very good, mild gingersnap.

Pepparkakor (Swedish Gingersnaps)

YIELD: ABOUT 7 DOZEN MEDIUM-SIZED COOKIES

4 ounces butter (½ stick)

4 ounces margarine (½ stick), suitable for baking

1½ cups white sugar

1 egg

1 tablespoon light corn syrup

¼ cup orange juice

2 teaspoons finely grated orange zest

3½ cups all-purpose flour

2 teaspoons baking soda

2 teaspoons ground cinnamon

2 teaspoons ground ginger

½ teaspoon ground cloves

FRESH SEASONINGS

Before I start to cook or bake a dish calling for spices and herbs, like the pepparkakor, I often invest in a small amount of fresh spices, especially if there's a place to buy them in bulk. In St. Paul I can get small amounts at my food co-op, the Mississippi Market, although more and more regular grocery stores are carrying bulk seasonings. Scooping out small quantities of fragrant herbs and spices into small plastic bags fills the air with the promise of the delicious dish to follow.

In a large bowl, cream butter, margarine and sugar till sugar is completely incorporated. Stir in egg, corn syrup, orange juice and orange zest. Sift together flour, baking soda, cinnamon, ginger and cloves. Stir into the creamed mixture until completely combined. Chill dough, covered, in refrigerator 4 to 6 hours.

When you're ready to bake, preheat oven to 400°F. Roll out dough to ⅛-inch-thickness and cut into shapes with cookie cutters. Place on lightly greased cookie sheets about one inch apart. Bake 8 to 10 minutes until the cookies just begin to turn brown around the edges. Cool cookies on wire racks.

THE SECRET TO ROLLING OUT COOKIES EASILY

I roll out the dough between two sheets of waxed paper that I've sprinkled with some white flour. Peel back the top sheet carefully when dough is ⅛-inch thick. Cut out cookies, placing the cookie cutters as near as possible to each other to get the most cuttings from the first rolling out. Form remaining scraps into a ball and refrigerate again until firm. Otherwise, in a warm kitchen like mine with a 400°F oven turned on, the raw cookies will be too soft to keep their shape while you transfer them from the waxed paper to the cookie sheet.

Yulekage, Julekage, Julekake—you'll see recipes in upper Midwest cookbooks that use a variety of spellings, sometimes one word, sometimes two. They're all variants of a much-loved seasonal yeast bread that many Scandinavian Americans prefer to fruitcake. This recipe appeared in Minneapolis's Norwegian Lutheran Memorial Church's *Cookbook of Tested Recipes.* It's almost as good toasted as it is fresh!

Julekake (Norwegian Christmas Bread)

MRS. J. O. BJORDAL

YIELD: MAKES 3 LARGE LOAVES

NOTE: You'll find citron in the fruitcake section of grocery stores in November and December.

1¼ cups milk, divided

½ cup butter

½ cup plus 1 tablespoon sugar, divided

1 teaspoon salt

1 package instant rapid rise yeast

¼ cup warm water

4 to 5 cups bread flour

¼ teaspoon fresh ground cardamom

½ cup raisins

2 ounces chopped citron (see Note)

1 egg yolk

Scald 1 cup of the milk in a saucepan, heating until small bubbles form around the side. Add butter, ½ cup of the sugar and the salt, stirring until the butter is melted and the sugar is dissolved. Set aside to cool to lukewarm. While the milk mixture is cooling, proof the yeast by mixing it with the warm water and the remaining 1 tablespoon of the sugar. Set it aside until the mixture is foaming, a sign that the yeast will work.

Put 2 cups of the flour in a large mixing bowl, add the milk and yeast mixtures and stir until well blended. Next add the cardamom, raisins, citron and 2 more cups of the flour. Work this with your hands, adding more flour as needed and kneading until you have a soft dough that is not sticky. Place dough in a large, clean, lightly greased bowl and cover with a damp cloth. Set aside in a warm place to rise until double. This could take about an hour or longer. Punch dough down, form into two or three oblong loaves and place them on lightly greased cookie sheets. Be sure to allow plenty of room for the loaves to rise. Set aside to rise until double once again; this could take another 30 to 45 minutes.

When ready to bake, preheat oven to 350°F. Beat egg yolk with remaining ¼ cup of the milk and brush lightly on top of loaves. Bake until loaves are light brown and sound hollow when tapped, about 45 to 60 minutes, depending on size of loaves.

This recipe comes from *Swanington's Treasure of Personal Recipes,* Swanington, Indiana, compiled by the Ladies Aid of the Evangelical United Brethren Church.

Bohemian Mashed Banana Cake

MRS. SYLVESTER GARING

YIELD: 1 (13×9-INCH) CAKE, SERVING 20 OR MORE

NOTE: Have all ingredients at room temperature, especially butter and eggs. I use large eggs for baking, rather than medium or extra-large.

1 tablespoon vinegar	3 cups flour
1 cup milk	1 teaspoon baking powder
½ cup butter	1 scant teaspoon baking soda
2 cups sugar	pinch of salt
3 large ripe bananas, mashed	1 cup chopped walnuts or pecans
2 eggs, well beaten	

Preheat oven to 350°F. Grease a 13×9×2½-inch pan (see page 113 for tips). Combine vinegar with milk and let stand about 3 minutes to make soured milk. Cream butter and sugar until fluffy. Add mashed bananas and mix well. Stir in beaten eggs. Sift flour with baking powder, soda and salt. Add to banana mixture, alternating with soured milk, about a third of each at a time, beginning and ending with flour mixture. Stir in chopped nuts.

Pour batter into pan. Bake 40 to 50 minutes until cake is golden brown and firm in the center and pulled slightly away from the sides. Turn pan once in oven after 20 minutes to ensure even baking.

This recipe comes from *The Mixing Bowl*, published by the North Methodist Church Wesleyan Service Guild, Minneapolis.

Glorified Rice

MRS. WARREN E. NELSON

SERVES 8 TO 10

1 cup whipping cream

1 teaspoon vanilla

2 tablespoons sugar

1 (14- to 16-ounce) can crushed pineapple

10 to 12 marshmallows, quartered, or 40 to 50 miniature marshmallows

3 cups cooked white rice

Whip cream and add vanilla and sugar. Put into a big bowl and add pineapple with liquid, marshmallows and rice, mix well. Chill in refrigerator.

The now-famous Minnesota cookbook author Bea Ojakangas contributed this recipe to *Curriculum for Cooks,* a 1958 cookbook compiled by the University of Minnesota Hospitals Auxiliary and the Faculty Women's Club. It is used here with her permission.

This is a great recipe for those who really like "hands-on" cooking. You can use either fresh or frozen blueberries. If you get out this summer and pick enough berries to freeze some, try this buttery bar with the up-north flavor of those berries. Packaged frozen berries are pretty good these days too. Don't thaw them, just knock off any ice crystals.

Finnish Blueberry Dessert

BEA OJAKANGAS

YIELD: 24 (3×2-INCH) BARS

CRUST AND TOP STRIPS
2¼ cups flour
½ cup sugar
½ teaspoon baking powder
1 cup butter

FILLING:
½ to 1 cup sugar, to taste
1 tablespoon cornstarch
dash of salt
3 cups blueberries, washed and dried if fresh

Preheat oven to 425°F. Grease a 16×12-inch jellyroll pan before baking (see page 113 for tips). Combine flour, sugar and baking powder in a large mixing bowl. Cut the butter into small pieces and work into the flour mixture with your fingers until the butter is thoroughly incorporated into the dry ingredients—about 5 minutes. You will have a rich buttery dough that holds together. Set aside about 1 cup of the dough for the top strips.

Press the rest of the dough onto the bottom of the jellyroll pan. Make sure the dough is evenly distributed across the entire pan and forms a firm crust. Roll out the remaining 1 cup of dough between 2 sheets of lightly floured waxed paper with a rolling pin until it's a thin rectangle, about ⅛-inch thick. Carefully peel off the top piece of waxed paper, repairing any tears in the dough with your fingers as you go along. Cut diagonally into ½-inch-wide strips of varying lengths.

Mix the sugar, cornstarch and salt. Toss the blueberries with this dry mixture. Spread coated berries evenly over the bottom crust. Top with dough strips in a lattice or simple stripe pattern. If dough breaks when you pick it up from the wax paper with a thin spatula, don't worry. Patch it together and it will bake into a single strip.

Bake for 20 to 25 minutes, or until strips and visible edges are golden brown.

BARS and COOKIES

Rae Katherine Eighmey

RECIPE FOR A CHILD AT PLAY

Take one small child;
Mix liberally with boxes, boards, a little rope,
and a pail or two;
Add a reasonable facsimile of dad's
or mother's old hat,
And a pair of Grandpa's spectacle frames.
Throw in a couple of old scrub brushes,
a cast-off necktie or two—Or Mom's old skirt.

Add a good sturdy wagon if one is available.
Season each with love and understanding.
Stir in lightly a good sense of humor.
Sprinkle liberally with dirt and water.
Turn out in a side yard with a
companion or two.

Like a good cake this mixture takes
a light hand, a watchful eye,
But not too much prying and poking,
And little or no heat.

DOROTHEA CONKLIN, *ADVENTURES IN THE KITCHEN,*
WOMEN OF WAVERLY LUTHERAN CHURCH, TRUMAN, MN (1954)

Though I grew up in Indiana, I had never seen these bars using my state's nickname. But I certainly am glad Mrs. Robert Hasset from Two Harbors, Minnesota, put them into the Methodist church cookbook. The combination of sweet meringue layer between chocolate and salty peanut accents is unusual and very good. One tradition has it that "Hoosier" began as a mispronunciation of "Who's here?"—words called out by travelers as they passed. If these bars had been on the table, they would have moved right in.

Hoosier Bars

YIELD: 36 (2×1½-INCH) BARS

½ cup shortening or butter
½ cup white sugar
1½ cups brown sugar, firmly packed, divided
2 eggs, separated
3 tablespoons cold water
1 teaspoon vanilla
2 cups bread flour
2 teaspoons baking powder
1 teaspoon baking soda
1 cup chocolate chips
3 to 4 ounces finely chopped salted peanuts

Preheat oven to 325°F. Line a 13×9-inch pan with foil and spray with non-stick cooking spray; set aside. Cream shortening, white sugar and ½ cup of the brown sugar. Add egg yolks, water and vanilla. Mix until smooth. Add flour, baking powder and baking soda and mix well. Smooth batter into pan. Sprinkle chocolate chips on top. Then in a perfectly clean bowl with grease-free beaters, beat the 2 egg whites till stiff. Gradually add remaining 1 cup of the brown sugar. Continue beating until egg whites are glossy and stiff. Spread over chips and then sprinkle with salted peanuts. Bake 30 to 35 minutes. Cool, lift bars in foil out of pan, carefully peel foil back and cut into bars.

BEATING EGG WHITES AND MAKING MERINGUE

Although beaten egg whites provide remarkable structure to baked goods, getting them to that stage can be tricky. You need perfectly clean, grease-free beaters and bowl. The slightest speck of yolk will keep them from forming the high peaks you want. Break each egg over a small bowl first so that if the yolk mixes with a white, you can save that one for scrambled eggs. Room temperature eggs whip better. Put the eggs in a bowl of lukewarm water for 5 minutes or so before you crack them. Beat the egg whites at low speed until they get frothy. For increased stability you may add about an 1/8 teaspoon cream of tartar at this point and continue to beat at low speed until this is dissolved. Then beat at high speed, and if you are making meringue begin adding the sugar one tablespoon at a time.

U sing dry oatmeal instead of part or all of the flour in the crust for either of these bars gives them a nutty flavor and texture and a healthful aspiration. Both bars are really good too.

Apricot Bars

YIELD: 36 (2×1½-INCH) BARS

1 cup brown sugar, firmly packed
1½ cup sifted flour
1 teaspoon baking powder
¾ cup shortening or cold butter
1½ cups quick-cooking oats, not instant
1 cup apricot jam

Preheat oven to 350°F. Grease a 13×9×2-inch baking pan before baking (see page 113 for tips). Combine sugar, flour and baking powder in a large mixing bowl. Cut in shortening with a pastry cutter or two knives until it resembles cornmeal. Stir in the quick oats. Divide mixture in thirds. Press ⅔ of the mixture into the bottom of the pan. Stir apricot jam to soften slightly and spread carefully over firmly packed crust mixture. Cover jam with remaining oats mixture and press gently into place. Bake 35 minutes or until brown. Cool and cut in bars.

Scotch Toffee Bars

YIELD: 24 (2×2-INCH) BARS

NOTE: This recipe does not use any flour.

½ cup melted butter

2 cups quick-cooking oats, not instant

½ cup brown sugar, firmly packed

¼ cup dark corn syrup

½ teaspoon salt

1½ teaspoons vanilla

1 cup chocolate chips

¼ cup chopped walnuts

Preheat oven to 350°F. Grease an 11×8-inch pan before baking (see page 113 for tips). Pour melted butter over oats and mix thoroughly. Add brown sugar, corn syrup, salt and vanilla, stirring with a spoon until well blended. Pack firmly into pan. Bake for 15 minutes or until rich golden brown. Crust will appear very bubbly when you take it out of the oven. Turn oven off and let the crust cool about 5 minutes; sprinkle chocolate chips on top and return to the oven for one minute to begin melting the chips. Gently spread melting chips all over the crust. Sprinkle with nuts. Cool completely before cutting into bars with a sharp knife.

W e found scores of Dream Bar variations to test. It was like living some high-calorie version of Goldilocks. This one was too sweet. This one was too dry. Finally, this one was just right.

Dream Bars

YIELD: 36 (1½ BY 2-INCH) BARS

CRUST:

½ cup butter

¼ cup brown sugar, firmly packed

1 cup flour

FROSTING:

1½ cup powdered sugar

2 tablespoons butter, very soft

2 tablespoons orange juice

1 tablespoon lemon juice

FILLING:

½ cup coconut

1½ cups brown sugar

1 cup chopped nuts

2 tablespoons flour

¼ teaspoon baking powder

¼ teaspoon salt

2 eggs, lightly beaten

1 teaspoon vanilla

Preheat oven to 350°F. Grease a 12×9×2-inch pan before baking (see page 113 for tips). Make the crust by creaming ½ cup butter and ¼ cup brown sugar together. Add 1 cup flour and mix well. Spread batter into the pan. Bake until crust is firm and just beginning to brown, about 12 to 15 minutes. When crust is almost done, make the filling. Combine coconut, brown sugar, nuts, flour, baking powder and salt. Stir eggs lightly with vanilla. Add to the dry ingredients and mix thoroughly. Pour over the baked crust and return to the oven. Bake until firm, about 20 to 25 minutes. Remove from oven and cool on a wire rack. When bars are completely cool, frost with mixture of powdered sugar, butter and juices.

GETTING GOODIES OUT OF PANS NEATLY

Baking pan preparation used to be simple. Smoosh a generous coating of butter or shortening all over the inside of the baking pan, sprinkle well with flour, turn the pan upside down and knock out the extra, then set the pan aside until ready to put the batter in and bake. That method still works. Just be certain any shortening or margarine you use is suitable for baking—many table spreads have a high water content and will not work. I have started using non-stick sprays instead. Sprays that combine fat and flour work the same as grease and flour, but I have better luck with the pure oil ones if I spray the pan immediately before I put the batter or dough into it. If you do it any sooner, the spray tends to collect in droplets and isn't as effective.

Heavy-duty aluminum foil is my best friend for liberating bars from their pans. Line the baking pan with foil, and grease that instead of greasing the pan. When the bars are baked you can lift them out of the pan in one piece, peel the foil back and cut neatly into squares for serving. Foil is also very handy for making baking pans smaller. If, for example, you don't have an 8-inch square pan, you can shrink a 9-inch pan by folding in a doubled edge of the foil an inch on two sides.

Refrigerator Cookies

Grown people who know better reached for thirds and fourths when we passed icebox cookie samples. To a person they said, "I haven't had these in years!" Some preferred the date spirals, others the chocolate pinwheels. I like the basic butterscotch best. Keep a log or two of these easy-to-make doughs well wrapped in your freezer and you'll have delicious cookies to pop fresh into the oven. The oddities of dough slumping into less than perfect rounds in the refrigerator give them unforgettable character.

Butterscotch Icebox Cookies

YIELD: 8 DOZEN COOKIES

2 cups brown sugar, firmly packed
1 cup melted butter
2 eggs
1 teaspoon vanilla
1 teaspoon cream of tartar
1 teaspoon baking soda
4 cups flour
1 cup finely chopped walnuts

Stir the sugar, butter, eggs and vanilla together until completely blended. Add the dry ingredients, mixing thoroughly, and then stir in the chopped walnuts. Divide the dough in half and form each half into a log about 1 inch high and 2 inches wide. Wrap each log in plastic wrap. Chill at least 2 hours.

When ready to bake, preheat the oven to 375°F. Grease baking sheets. Slice dough about ⅛-inch thick with a very sharp knife. Place slices on baking sheets about 2 inches apart. Bake until lightly browned, about 10 to 12 minutes.

Pinwheel Icebox Cookies

YIELD: 6 DOZEN COOKIES

¼ cup butter, at room temperature

⅔ cup sugar

1 egg yolk, lightly beaten

3 tablespoons milk

½ teaspoon vanilla

1½ cups flour

1½ teaspoons baking powder

¼ teaspoon salt

1 square unsweetened chocolate, melted, or 2 tablespoons cocoa powder

Cream butter and sugar; stir in egg yolk, milk and vanilla. Add the dry ingredients, mixing thoroughly. Divide the dough in half. On a piece of waxed paper or plastic wrap, roll out half of the dough about ¼-inch thick and into a rectangle of about 15×10 inches. Combine chocolate or cocoa powder with the remaining half of the dough. Roll that half out on a sheet of waxed paper or plastic wrap to the same size as the vanilla layer. Flip the chocolate layer onto the white layer, press gently all over and then remove the waxed paper. Using the waxed paper under the white layer as an aid, tightly roll the dough into a log to form the pinwheel design. Pull the paper away from the dough as you roll and discard. Wrap the log in plastic wrap or foil and chill at least 2 hours.

When ready to bake, preheat the oven to 350°F. Grease baking sheets. Slice dough into ⅛-inch-thick slices and place on baking sheets about 2 inches apart. Bake until lightly browned, about 10 to 12 minutes.

Date-Filled Icebox Cookies

YIELD: 6 DOZEN COOKIES

FILLING:

1 pound pitted dates

½ cup white sugar

½ cup water

COOKIE DOUGH:

1 cup shortening or butter at room temperature

1 cup white sugar

1 cup brown sugar, firmly packed

3 eggs

1 teaspoon vanilla

1 teaspoon baking soda

4 cups flour

COOKING WITH DATES

Most grocery stores sell pitted dates in 8-ounce packages in the baking or dried-fruit aisle. They come chopped or whole. I prefer using the whole dates and cutting them up. Most chopped dates are dusted with sugar and will remain whole in baked goods, and in these 1950s recipes, dates need to cook down to a smooth jam. It is worth having a pair of scissors get sticky in order to cut them yourself.

First make the date filling. If they are not already diced, cut dates into small pieces. Combine with ½ cup white sugar and water in a small saucepan. Cook over medium heat, stirring occasionally, until the dates fall apart, making a jam-like mixture. Set aside to cool. To make the dough, cream butter with white and brown sugars. Add the eggs and vanilla, mixing well. Stir in the baking soda and flour. Cover work surface with waxed paper or plastic wrap and roll the dough out ¼-inch thick into a rectangle approximately 18×10 inches. Carefully spread the cooled date jam over the cookie dough. Then, using the paper or wrap as an aid, roll the dough up from the long side, making a spiral of date filling. Wrap this dough log in plastic wrap and chill for at least 2 hours.

When ready to bake, preheat oven to 350°F. Grease baking sheets. Cut across roll in ¼-inch slices with a very sharp knife. Place on baking sheets and bake until golden brown, about 12 to 15 minutes. Cool on a wire rack.

> **A house
> is not a home by far
> if it has
> an empty cookie jar.**
> SYMPHONY OF COOKING, ST. LOUIS [MISSOURI]
> SYMPHONY SOCIETY (1954)

When I was in junior high I did some of my homework in the living room while watching old black-and-white movies played with lots of commercials. I remember seeing a few of Sonja Henie's films. An Olympic champion ice skater, she filled the small screen with grace and a cheerful, dimpled smile. She was born in Norway and became an American citizen in the early 1950s. Her charm, skills and movie presence no doubt helped build interest in the sport. I know my dad built a skating rink in the backyard. He ran a hose out the basement window, flooding the area within the snow edges he firmed up with a shovel so I could practice.

Sonja Henie Cookies

YIELD: 4 DOZEN COOKIES

1 cup butter, at room temperature
½ cup brown sugar, firmly packed
2 eggs, separated
2 cups flour
¾ cup almonds or walnuts, finely chopped
raspberry or lingonberry jam, optional

Preheat oven to 325°F. Cream butter and sugar. Blend in the egg yolks only, beating until light. Add flour and mix well. Lightly whisk the egg whites in a shallow bowl to break them up. Put chopped nuts into another shallow bowl. Roll pieces of dough into small balls about an inch in diameter. Roll each ball in egg whites and then in nuts. Place on lightly greased baking sheet about 2 inches apart. Make about a ¼-inch deep "thumbprint" dimple in the top of each cookie by gently pressing with finger or thumb. Bake until lightly browned, about 20 minutes. Cool on wire racks. You may fill the depression with a dab of raspberry or lingonberry jam, but these cookies are delightful just plain.

Not being a member of the Daughters of the American Revolution, I don't know why these are called D.A.R. cookies. I did ask my friend Ruth, a member in good standing. She had never seen cookies like these in her Nebraska and Iowa chapters. The directions are quite specific: cut with a circular cutter and place the cherry in the center. Some D.A.R. sashes have ribbon rosettes at the hip—maybe that is the connection. This is a lovely roll-out cookie even if we don't know any of the branches on its family tree.

D.A.R. Cookies

YIELD: 6 DOZEN COOKIES

⅔ cup butter, at room temperature
1½ cups white sugar
2 eggs
2 teaspoons vanilla
3 cups flour
1 teaspoon baking soda
2 teaspoons cream of tartar
2 tablespoons sweet milk, more or less
Candied cherries

Preheat oven to 350°F. Cream butter and sugar. Add eggs and vanilla, beating well to combine. Sift dry ingredients together and add to creamed mixture. At this point the dough may be the proper consistency to roll out. If it is too dry, add milk a teaspoon at a time until the dough is firm, pliable and not sticky. Divide the dough into fourths. Lightly dust rolling surface with flour. Roll out ¼ of the dough until about ⅛-inch thick. Cut with circular cutter, and place cookies on lightly greased baking sheet. Put a candied cherry slice in center of each. Repeat with rest of the dough. Bake until cookies are just light brown, about 10 to 12 minutes.

These two cookies got the highest ratings from our taste testers. They are easy to make, keep well, and have flavors and textures that transport us back to childhood, whether it is fifteen or fifty years ago. They are good grandma/grandkid cookies too. Rolling the dough balls between your palms to get them perfectly round, then dipping or rolling in sugar, is a great introduction to baking.

Molasses Ginger Cookie with Crackled Top

YIELD: 8 DOZEN COOKIES

¾ cup shortening or butter at room temperature
1¼ cup sugar, divided
1 egg, lightly beaten
¼ cup molasses
1 teaspoon ginger
1 teaspoon salt
1 teaspoon cinnamon
½ teaspoon nutmeg
½ teaspoon cloves
2 teaspoons baking soda
2 cups sifted flour

Preheat oven to 350°F. Cream shortening and 1 cup of the sugar. Add egg and molasses, beating well. Mix in spices and baking soda, followed by the flour. Form the dough into small balls about ¾ inch in diameter. Dip the top of each ball into remaining ¼ cup of the sugar. Place on lightly greased baking sheets about 2 inches apart. Bake until cookies are lightly browned on the edges and the top has crinkled, about 10 to 12 minutes.

Snickerdoodles

YIELD: 8 DOZEN COOKIES

1 cup soft shortening or butter
1½ cups plus 2 tablespoons sugar, divided
2 eggs
2¾ cups flour
2 teaspoons cream of tartar
1 teaspoon baking soda
½ teaspoon salt
2 teaspoons cinnamon

Cream shortening and 1½ cups of the sugar. Add eggs and beat well. Add flour, cream of tartar, baking soda and salt; mix until dough is smooth. Cover bowl with plastic wrap or place dough in an air-tight container and chill for at least 2 hours.

When ready to bake, preheat oven to 375°F. To make the coating mixture, combine remaining 2 tablespoons of the sugar and the cinnamon in a shallow bowl. Take small pieces of dough and roll between your palms into balls about ¾ inch in diameter. Then roll the balls in the coating mix and place 2 inches apart on lightly greased baking sheets. Bake until cookies just begin to turn brown around the edges and the centers are firm, about 8 to 10 minutes. Cool on a wire rack.

DESSERTS

Rae Katherine Eighmey

When I married my lean Jim,
I vowed I'd put some meat on him;
I fed him creams and pie and cake
All the victuals it could take—
He did not change from lean to stout,
And it wasn't long till I found out
That thinness was to be his fate,
And I had put on all the weight.

*THE MIXING BOWL, WESLEYAN SERVICE GUILD,
NORTH METHODIST CHURCH, MINNEAPOLIS, MN (1950)*

We wanted to include recipes for a pie or two in this collection. Apple, cherry, rhubarb—the cookbooks had standard recipes. Nothing special caught our attention until we found this oddly named pie in the *Evangelical United Brethren Treasury of Personal Recipes* from Swanington, Indiana. Certainly Mrs. George Mann of Otterbein, Indiana, knew what she was doing with eggs and two tablespoons of spices. The filling separates as it bakes, creating a lovely transparent layer topped with a spicy froth. Yum!

Bob Andy Pie

YIELD: 2 (8-INCH) PIES, SERVING 16

⅔ cup very soft butter

2 cups sugar

3 tablespoons flour

3 eggs, separated

1 tablespoon nutmeg

1 tablespoon cinnamon

2 cups milk

2 9-inch pie crusts

Preheat oven to 425°F. Mix butter, sugar, flour and the egg yolks. Add spices and milk; mix thoroughly. Beat the egg whites until they form stiff peaks and fold in. Pour mixture into unbaked crusts. Bake 15 minutes at 425°F, then reduce temperature to 350°F and bake until done, 25 to 30 minutes, until a knife put in the center comes out clean.

CUTTING RECIPES IN HALF

If you want to make only one of these pies, it is easy to cut most of the ingredients by half. However, the eggs are a challenge. Separate the eggs, then beat the yolks and whites separately just to break them up. Measure each and divide in half. Save the remaining portions for scrambled eggs.

The key to perfectly flaky pie crust is having all the ingredients cold. Cold butter or shortening, ice cold water—some cooks even chill the flour. I don't go that far. I've used my mother's pie crust recipe since I was ten.

Perfect Pie Crust

YIELD: 2 (9-INCH) CRUSTS

1½ cups flour	½ cup cold butter or shortening
½ teaspoon salt	4 to 6 tablespoons ice water

Combine flour and salt. Cut in butter with a pastry cutter until it looks like oatmeal. Sprinkle 4 tablespoons water onto mixture and blend with a fork. If dough is too dry, add more water by teaspoons until you have a dough that holds together. Don't handle too much. Roll out between sheets of waxed paper.

CUTTING IN FOR PERFECT PIE CRUST

Pastry cutter, food processor, two knives, or fingertips—all have been suggested over the years as a way to cut fat into small bits and simultaneously coat those bits with flour for pie crust or crumble toppings. All of these methods will work. My favorite is the pastry cutter. I happen to like best the heavy-gauge wire one I've used for more than forty years. Within two or three minutes I have nice pillows of fat and flour. I'm not as adept with the knives, and I think the food processor heats the fat a bit too much, as do fingers. The secret to baking a flaky crust is to have the fat melt within its coating of flour, releasing steam as it does. Make enough pies and you'll find the way that works best for you. Besides—you and the ones you love will get to eat some really fine test products along the way.

This pie appeared with several names. It is essentially an upside-down lemon meringue pie. The meringue forms the pie crust and is filled with the lemon curd.

Heavenly Pie

SERVES 8 TO 10

4 eggs, separated
¼ teaspoon cream of tartar
1½ cups sugar, divided
3 tablespoons shredded coconut, optional
3 tablespoons lemon juice
1 tablespoon grated lemon rind
Sweetened whipped cream

Preheat oven to 275°F. Beat the egg whites at low speed until frothy, then add cream of tartar. Continue beating on low until it dissolves; then increase speed and begin adding 1 cup of the sugar very gradually. Continue beating until egg whites are glossy and form stiff peaks. Spoon this meringue into an ungreased 9-inch pie plate. Sprinkle with coconut if desired. Bake 1 hour until firm. Remove from oven and cool.

While pie shell is baking, make the lemon filling. Beat the egg yolks until thick and light. Add remaining ½ cup of the sugar and continue beating until dissolved. Stir in lemon juice and rind. Cook in a double boiler over hot water until thick, stirring constantly. Cool, stirring from time to time so that a skin does not form on the top. Spoon cooled filling into cool meringue shell and top with sweetened whipped cream when ready to serve. Store pie without whipped cream, lightly covered, in the refrigerator. It lasts nicely for twenty-four hours.

each pies made with peach halves arranged over a filling appear everywhere in 1950s community cookbooks. They must have been potluck favorites and they are favorites in our kitchens now.

Peach Crumble Pie

SERVES 8

1 cup sugar

⅔ cup flour

⅛ teaspoon nutmeg

½ cup cold butter

3 to 4 large fresh peaches

1 unbaked 9-inch pie crust at least 1½ inches deep

¼ cup water

Preheat oven to 425°F. Mix sugar, flour and nutmeg in a small mixing bowl. Using a pastry cutter, cut butter into sugar and flour until crumbly, about the size of oatmeal. Cut peaches in half, peel and remove the pit. Sprinkle half of the crumbs into the pie crust. Working around the edge of the pie crust, arrange peach halves cut-side down over crumbs. Cut halves into pieces to fill center if necessary. Cover with remaining crumb mixture. Gently pour water over the top and bake at 425°F for 10 minutes. Lower heat to 350°F and bake until juices are bubbling and crumbs are golden, about 30 minutes longer.

Our taste testers said that this was the best gingerbread they had ever had. The original recipe suggested that "raisins and nuts are good in ginger bread. It may be iced with chocolate or other icing or served plain." But we all agreed that to add anything to it (even icing!) would be a shame.

Old-Fashioned Gingerbread

SERVES ABOUT 12

½ cup butter

1 cup sugar

2 eggs, lightly beaten

1 cup molasses

3 cups flour

2 teaspoons baking soda

2 teaspoons ginger

2 teaspoons cinnamon

1 teaspoon nutmeg

1 teaspoon allspice

¼ teaspoon cloves

1 cup buttermilk or sour milk

Preheat oven to 350°F (325°F for dark or glass pans). Grease a 9×4×4-inch loaf pan or 3 mini-loaf pans before baking (see page 113 for tips). Cream butter and sugar, then add eggs and molasses. Sift flour, baking soda and spices 3 times and add alternately with buttermilk, beginning and ending with flour mixture and beating hard after each addition. Pour batter into large loaf pan or divide among mini-loaf pans. Bake until gingerbread pulls away from the side of the pan and a knife or skewer inserted into the center comes out clean, about 65 minutes for large loaf pan or 55 minutes for mini-loaves.

In some of the cookbooks we looked at this is called "Lazy Daisy Cake," as it is quickly mixed and finished off with a broiled topping. The cake is a basic hot milk sponge cake, one of the classic cake recipes. I like to think of it not only as a quick everyday cake, but as a terrific lake cabin treat. It is warm and chewy—equally good for breakfast as well as a moonlight dessert.

Hot Coconut-Covered Cake

YIELD: 1 CAKE, SERVING ABOUT 9

CAKE:

1 cup flour

1 teaspoon baking powder

2 eggs

1 cup sugar

1 tablespoon butter

½ cup hot milk

Preheat oven to 350°F. Grease a 9×9-inch pan before baking (see page 113 for tips). Combine flour and baking powder, sift and set aside. With an electric mixer, beat eggs until they are light and lemon-colored. This could take as long as 5 minutes. Gradually add sugar, beating continually. Add butter to hot milk. Stir the flour mixture into the eggs. Then quickly beat in milk and butter. Pour batter into pan. Bake until cake is golden brown and firm in the center, about 25 minutes. Cool cake until just warm and then finish off with topping.

TOPPING:

6 tablespoons melted butter

⅔ cup brown sugar, firmly packed

¼ cup cream

1 cup coconut

1 teaspoon vanilla

Combine ingredients. Spread over slightly cooled cake. Put cake under the broiler on a rack in the middle of the oven, at least 5 inches below broiler flame. Broil for 3 to 5 minutes. Watch carefully or it will burn. Serve warm.

Talk about the fear of being judged. State Fair food contests are nothing compared to the pressure of being the last cake selected at the PTA Fundraiser Cake Walk. Every mom would bring a home-baked cake. No mixes or—pass the smelling salts—bakery cakes allowed. The rules varied from school to school, but the contest is sort of like musical chairs. You had to buy a ticket for a quarter. Music would play, music would stop and you'd scramble for a chair. Each chair had a number on it and the dad running the game would reach in and pull out a number. If you were sitting in that chair, you got to go up to the table—here the drama and tension begins—and pick a cake. Woe to the mom whose cake stood there round after round. Chocolate layer cakes went fast and so did easy-to-tote-home variations of pound cake like this one.

Sour Cream Nut Cake

SERVES 10 TO 12

½ cup chopped walnuts

1¾ cups cake flour

1 teaspoon baking powder

½ teaspoon baking soda

⅛ teaspoon salt

½ cup butter

1 cup sugar

2 eggs

1 cup sour cream

1 teaspoon vanilla

Preheat the oven to 350°F. Grease a tube pan or 4 mini-loaf pans before baking (see page 113 for tips). Toast the walnuts on a baking sheet in the oven until lightly browned. Chop very finely and set aside. Sift cake flour, baking powder, baking soda and salt together and set aside. Cream butter and sugar, add eggs and beat until well mixed. Stir in sour cream and vanilla. Add chopped walnuts, and then fold in sifted dry ingredients. Pour batter into tube pan or divide among mini-loaf pans. Bake until light brown and firm in the center. A tube pan will take about 40 to 50 minutes, mini-loaf pans about 30 to 40 minutes.

Ahhh—low-fat ice cream simply made in the refrigerator freezer. I remember mixing up the lemon version of this dessert treat in the morning, stirring it at noon and serving it at supper. Nice and light. A lovely treat served with a simple pound cake.

Pineapple Milk Sherbet

YIELD: ABOUT 8 (½-CUP) SERVINGS

1½ cups crushed pineapple
2 cups milk, low fat or nonfat
1 cup sugar
juice of half a lemon
juice of half an orange

Mix all ingredients. Stir until sugar is dissolved. Freeze until half frozen then beat with wooden spoon until smooth. Refreeze until firm.

I remember the late 1950s as a time of science and a space race in the midst of the Cold War. Russia launched Sputnik, the world's first artificial satellite, into outer space in October 1957. In response, American schools started emphasizing science, and my kid brother successfully made loads of model rockets. Alas, the U.S. rocket program didn't go together as simply. Many mornings we awoke before dawn to watch televised launches of Vanguard rockets with our fingers crossed, only to have the countdown go into a hold or, worse yet, the rocket explode on the launch pad. Finally, with the successful launch of Explorer 1 in 1958, we were in the race.

Certainly this dessert could be thought of as a science experiment in a cake pan, and it is a success every time.

Crazy Chocolate Cake

SERVES 8

1½ cups sifted flour

1 cup sugar

1 teaspoon baking soda

3 tablespoons cocoa powder

½ teaspoon salt

⅓ cup all-purpose vegetable oil such as Wesson

1 tablespoon vinegar

1 teaspoon vanilla

1 cup milk

Preheat oven to 350°F. Sift flour, sugar, baking soda, cocoa powder and salt into an ungreased 8×8-inch pan. Make three depressions in these ingredients. Put oil in one, vinegar in another and vanilla in the third. Gently pour milk over the entire pan and carefully stir with a fork until ingredients are well blended into a slightly lumpy batter. Bake until cake is firm in the center, about 25 to 30 minutes. Cool and frost with Chocolate Cream Frosting.

Chocolate Cream Frosting

YIELD: ENOUGH TO FROST 2 (8×8-INCH) CAKES

NOTE: Divide recipe amounts in half for Crazy Chocolate Cake or store left-over frosting in refrigerator for up to a week.

3 tablespoons butter
3 squares unsweetened baking chocolate
1 cup brown sugar
½ cup water
2 to 3 cups sifted powdered sugar

In a 2-quart saucepan, melt butter and chocolate over low heat, stirring constantly. Add brown sugar and water, increase heat to medium and bring to boiling point, stirring from time to time. Boil 3 minutes. Remove from heat and let cool to lukewarm. Add enough sifted powdered sugar to make a spreading consistency.

first ran across a version of this dessert in *Gourmet* magazine in the late 1970s. Back then it quickly became our son's favorite dessert. It may have been that he had a particularly sophisticated taste for a 10-year-old. Or maybe he just liked having two desserts in one—cake and pudding. Finding the recipe in several of the 1950s cookbooks, I was amused and pleased to discover that what I thought was a sophisticated New York skyscraper recipe appeared twenty years earlier in midwestern church basements.

Lemon Sponge Pudding

SERVES 6

3 eggs, separated
pinch cream of tartar
¼ cup butter
¾ cup sugar
⅓ cup lemon juice
⅓ cup flour
1½ cups milk

Preheat oven to 350°F. Beat the egg whites until stiff with cream of tartar and set aside. Cream butter and sugar, add the egg yolks and lemon juice, mixing well to blend. Stir in flour. With the mixer running, add milk in a stream. Fold ¼ of the beaten egg whites into the batter, then fold in the rest. Pour batter into a buttered 1½-quart soufflé or casserole dish. Set the dish in a large pan of very hot water so that the water comes halfway up the side of the soufflé dish (see tip below). Bake until the pudding separates and the cake layer rises to the top, becomes firm and just starts to brown, about 50 minutes. Serve at room temperature. Refrigerate any leftovers and serve chilled the next day.

HOT WATER BATHS TO
TEMPER BAKING HEAT

Baked dishes with lots of eggs in them, such as custards, cook more evenly when they are protected from the direct heat of the oven. In this case, placing the soufflé dish in a large pan of very hot water that comes halfway up the sides lets the batter divide and gently form the bottom custard layer and the top light cake. It is much simpler and safer to put the soufflé dish in the larger pan, place them both on the oven rack and then carefully pour the hot water around the outside of the pudding dish. When the cake is finished, it is also safer to first carefully lift the soufflé dish out of the larger pan. The water level will drop and the pan will be much easier to take out of the oven without risk of boiling water spilling on the floor—or you.

Blueberries are a mythic fruit in our family and a special treat when we were kids. They were not nearly as common in 1950s grocery stores as they are today. We had friends who would drive to Michigan and return bearing trophy pints of U-Pick berries held high in their blue-stained fingers. My friend JB's favorite camp memory is of an early morning hike through north Minnesota woods to pick wild berries and cook pancakes over a campfire. More prosaically, a tiny taste of Gerber's blueberry buckle on the end of the spoon was enough to get the boring rice cereal past our daughter's discriminating baby palate. Not for nothing at the time her favorite picture book—and mine—was Robert McClusky's *Blueberries for Sal.* He wrote about Maine, but I prefer to think Sal and her mother got separated on a hill in Wisconsin, Michigan or Minnesota.

This blueberry buckle celebrates the essence of summer. During baking it makes a blueberry jam on top of a tender cake.

Blueberry Buckle

SERVES 9

1 pint blueberries

Wash the berries and pick through them to remove any spoiled ones and any lingering stems. Dry on paper toweling.

TOPPING:
½ cup sugar
⅓ cup flour
½ teaspoon cinnamon
¼ cup cold butter

Preheat oven to 350°F. Stir sugar, flour and cinnamon together in a small bowl. Cut in butter until crumbly. Set aside.

BUCKLE:

¼ cup soft butter

½ cup sugar

1 egg

1 cup flour

1½ teaspoons baking powder

¼ teaspoon salt

⅛ cup milk

Lightly grease a 9-inch square pan. Make the buckle. Cream butter and sugar well, add egg and beat well. Sift together flour, baking powder and salt. Add alternately with milk to first mixture. When mixed, pour into pan. Kerplunk the berries on top of the dough so a layer just one berry deep completely and evenly covers the batter. Sprinkle with topping. Bake until blueberries are bubbly around the edges and the topping is a light golden brown, about 25 to 30 minutes.

> The evening began with a dessert luncheon served to the twenty guests at card tables centered with candles and with each place marked by a pink bootie nut cup and a napkin shaped like a baby kimono.
>
> TRUMAN (MINNESOTA) INDEPENDENT, APRIL 5, 1951

FRIENDLY, FABULOUS, FIFTIES ENTERTAINING

Rae Katherine Eighmey

Memories, newspaper social notices, and the cookbooks we read gave us wonderful snapshots of 1950s social life. In the Midwest, especially in small towns, parties and entertainments were homemade affairs. Costume parties weren't confined to the last week of October. Amateur musicians brought instruments and voices to fill living rooms with song. Recitations of poetry or humorous commentary delighted neighbors. Demonstrations of skills or lectures on cultural topics informed study groups. Locally penned skits gently ribbed guests of honor.

The kitchen was the center of many a homemaker's life, as portrayed in the lines below from an anonymous Waverly poet. Foods ranged from ingredients quickly tossed together from the pantry to thoughtfully prepared menus. In this final chapter we've put together menus and we look back at some remembered festive events. Whether fast or fancy, the dishes are delightful and worthy of re-creating, as is the party atmosphere in which they were served.

> **My Kitchen**
> Here I may be a scientist
> Who measures as she makes.
> Here I may be an artist,
> Creating as she bakes.
> Here busy heart and brain and hand
> May feel and think and do.
> A kitchen is a happy place
> To make a dream come true.
> —ADVENTURES IN THE KITCHEN, WOMEN OF
> WAVERLY LUTHERAN CHURCH, 1954

Feeding the Multitudes

Ten pounds of ham makes 400 sandwiches, 20 pounds of chicken turns into chicken loaf for 48, a peck of potatoes mashes to feed 50, a gallon of salad satisfies 34 lodge members. Most of the cookbooks we looked at featured quantity cooking sections explaining how parish cooks provided good hearty food to please parishioners.

In my northern Indiana hometown, Presbyterian church annual dinners featured meatloaf and mashed potatoes, with the ladies of the church contributing desserts. The Catholics across the street had a fish fry during Lent. Dinner wasn't the only meal the "ladies of the church" prepared. One of our associates has vivid memories of lining up with his four siblings for homemade doughnuts after Mass at all-you-can-eat pancake breakfasts at Our Lady of Grace.

In Minnesota and the Dakotas the smorgasbord has a special place in church tradition. The annual Waverly smorgasbord featured meatballs, scalloped potatoes, Jell-O salads, relish plates, baked beans, cottage cheese, lefse, cookies and coffee. The Ladies of the Waverly Lutheran Church shared their recipe for these delicious meatballs. They kindly reduced the recipe from the 450 they typically serve to a mere 45. Go ahead and make the whole batch. They freeze beautifully.

Waverly Smorgasbord Meatballs

SERVES 45

1 cup finely minced onions
2 tablespoons butter
1 cup plain zwieback crumbs or dry bread crumbs
1 cup milk
5 pounds ground beef
1 pound ground pork

5 eggs, lightly beaten

1 teaspoon nutmeg

1 teaspoon pepper

5 teaspoons salt or less to taste

4 (10½-ounce) cans condensed consommé

½ cup flour

1 cup cold water

Preheat oven to 400°F. Cook onions in the butter until transparent. Crush zwieback and soak in milk. Mix together with ground beef, ground pork, eggs and seasonings. Form into balls the size of large walnuts. Place in cake pans or sheet pans that have an edge, lined with foil to make cleanup easier. Bake about 20 minutes until lightly browned and cooked through to an internal temperature of 160°F. Place meatballs and juices from the baking pan in large pot, cover with consommé, and simmer about 15 minutes. Remove meatballs and keep warm. Combine flour and water. Blend into cooking liquid and cook over low heat until gravy is thickened, stirring frequently.

THE MAGIC GRAVY JAR

A key piece of cooking equipment in my mother's kitchen was an old pint mayonnaise jar. It was the go-to tool for making gravy. The resulting sauce was largely low fat and thickened without lumps. The method is very simple. Measure flour into the jar, add very cold water, put the lid on tight, and shake very well. The flour and water slurry blends beautifully with stewing liquids—no need to make a butter and flour roux.

Delights for Drop-in Visitors

n countless midwestern cities, towns and villages, hospitality was an essential part of daily life. Casual morning visitors always received an offer of coffee, if not more. Afternoon and evening hostesses brought out spreads and dips to share with neighbors and friends.

The Lake Bronson, Minnesota, cookbook "committee" suggested this sandwich filling recipe to keep on hand for up to two weeks in the fridge. Today's safe food practices would suggest three days, tops.

Spicy Ham Spread

YIELD: ABOUT 2 CUPS, SERVING 6 TO 8

1 cup finely ground ham

⅛ cup finely chopped or ground pickle

⅛ cup chopped ripe olives

1 tablespoon minced parsley

1 tablespoon minced onion

1 tablespoon finely minced pimento

2 tablespoons brown sugar

½ teaspoon dry mustard

salt and pepper to taste

1 to 3 tablespoons mayonnaise

Combine all ingredients and chill until ready to spread as a sandwich filling or on crackers as an appetizer.

Crab Dip

YIELD: 2 CUPS, SERVING 6 TO 8

¾ cup sour cream

¼ cup mayonnaise

1 (6½-ounce) can crab meat,
    drained and flaked

1 tablespoon capers

1 tablespoon grated onion

1 tablespoon lemon juice

salt and pepper to tast

Combine all ingredients. Chill for
at least 2 hours. May be kept in
refrigerator for up to 24 hours.

Tasty Tomato Juice

YIELD: 5 (½-CUP) SERVINGS

18 ounces canned tomato juice

3 tablespoons lemon juice

1 teaspoon sugar

¼ teaspoon celery salt

1 teaspoon Worcestershire sauce

Combine all ingredients and serve
over ice.

PARTY PANTRY

In addition to prepared dips and spreads, tasteful hostesses in the 1950s always
had canned crab, shrimp and deviled ham, along with cheeses, salami, crackers,
Melba toast, pretzels, olives, pickles, cauliflower florets, celery and carrot sticks
and party rye bread on hand. Radish and tomato flowers enhanced snack trays.

Card Party Spaghetti Supper

Friends and relatives came to help Mrs. Martin Meyer celebrate her birthday Wednesday night. Five Hundred was played until 11 o'clock. . . . After the prizes were given, they all enjoyed spaghetti and meat sauce after midnight.

Most of the cookbooks we looked at featured "real Italian spaghetti," usually credited to someone's "real Italian friend." The number of seasonings, vegetables, and actual minced garlic set these recipes apart from the basic hamburger, tomato sauce or soup, salt and pepper version concocted in 1950s kitchens, including mine. Served with garlic bread, punch and birthday cake such as the recipe for the "new" German chocolate cake that follows, the Meyers' guests would have gone home quite happy.

Party Punch

YIELD: ABOUT 40 (½-CUP) SERVINGS

48 ounces unsweetened pineapple juice
1 cup lemon juice
1 cup orange juice
½ cup lime juice
1 cup sugar

2 quarts ginger ale
1 quart sparkling water
½ cup fresh mint leaves
1 cup sliced strawberries

Combine juices and stir in sugar until dissolved. Chill. When ready to serve, pour over ice in large punch bowl, add ginger ale, sparkling water, mint and strawberries.

Italian Spaghetti

SERVES 6 TO 8

2 tablespoons olive oil

1 pound ground beef

4 onions, chopped

2 green peppers, chopped

2 cloves garlic, minced

2 or 3 carrots, grated

1 (14- to 16-ounce) can tomatoes

2 (6-ounce) cans tomato paste
   (may use only one)

½ teaspoon salt

¼ teaspoon pepper

¼ teaspoon thyme

¼ teaspoon basil

¼ teaspoon oregano

¼ teaspoon marjoram

¼ teaspoon dry mustard

¼ teaspoon rosemary

1 bay leaf

1½ teaspoons paprika

red pepper to taste, about ⅛ teaspoon

1 cup water

½ pound fresh mushrooms

2 tablespoons butter

½ cup dry white wine

1 pound spaghetti, boiled

Put olive oil in a 4-quart pot over medium heat. Brown ground beef and then add onions, peppers and garlic. Sauté until peppers are limp and onions are transparent. Add carrots, tomatoes, tomato paste, seasonings and water. Simmer the sauce over very low heat at least 2 hours, stirring from time to time. Fifteen minutes before serving, sauté mushrooms in butter and add to sauce. Add wine at the last minute. Remove bay leaf and dispose of it. Serve over boiled spaghetti.

The original recipe for this cake said it was "new and delicious." It is a very interesting light chocolate cake that bakes in three 9-inch layers. With the rich chocolate frosting made from chocolate chips it is a spectacular dessert that can easily satisfy sixteen.

German Chocolate Cake

YIELD: 3 (9-INCH) CAKE LAYERS

NOTE: This cake goes from molten middle to burned edges faster than any other cake I've ever baked. Start checking at 20 minutes and don't leave the kitchen until you take the layers from the oven.

1 (4-ounce) German sweet baking-chocolate bar

5 eggs, separated

1 cup butter

2 cups sugar

1 teaspoon vanilla

1 teaspoon baking soda

2½ cups flour

1 cup buttermilk

Preheat oven to 350°F. Grease three 9-inch cake pans before baking (see page 113 for tips). Melt the chocolate over hot water or in the microwave. Separate eggs. Set the yolks aside and beat the egg whites until they form stiff peaks; set them aside to be added last. In a large mixing bowl, cream butter and sugar. Add the egg yolks one at a time and then the slightly cooled melted chocolate and vanilla. Add baking soda and 1 cup of the flour. Then add ½ cup of the buttermilk followed by another 1 cup of the flour, the remaining ½ cup of the buttermilk and the remaining ½ cup of the flour, mixing well after each addition. Fold in ⅓ of the beaten egg whites to lighten the batter and then fold in the remaining egg whites. Divide the batter among the 3 cake pans and bake until the layers are firm in the center and slightly pull away from the sides of the pans, about 20 to 25 minutes. Cool on wire rack and frost with Chocolate Icing.

Wonderful Chocolate Icing

YIELD: ABOUT 3 CUPS FROSTING, ENOUGH FOR A 3-LAYER (9-INCH) CAKE

1 cup semi-sweet chocolate chips

1 tablespoon butter

2 cups powdered sugar

6 tablespoons cream

2 teaspoons vanilla

Melt chocolate chips in a double boiler or in the microwave. Remove from heat. Add butter and mix well. Add half of the powdered sugar, then the cream followed by the remaining powdered sugar. Stir in vanilla. Beat until smooth and ready to spread. Add a bit more cream or sugar if necessary. Frost the tops of the layers with a thin layer of icing.

MELTING CHOCOLATE

Seized! The dreaded word while working with chocolate. Somewhere in the process of melting, it becomes hard, obnoxious and unmanageable. To avoid seizure, melt chocolate slowly. You can do it the old-fashioned way in the top of a double boiler over hot, but not boiling, water. If you don't have an actual double boiler, put a metal or heatproof ceramic bowl over the top of a saucepan of simmering water. The key is to have the water no hotter than a very slow simmer. Do not boil. Second, make sure the bottom of the chocolate container is not in direct contact with the water—"over, not in" is the watch phrase. Third, stir the chocolate as it melts, being careful not to burn yourself on the hot container. Finally, don't let any water get into the chocolate. You can also use a microwave to melt the chocolate. Start at 30 seconds at full power, then remove it and stir every 10 seconds. Once the chocolate begins to melt, take it out of the microwave and continue stirring. The container will usually retain enough heat to finish the job.

New Year's Eve Charade Elegance

Three words . . . Second word . . . Sounds like . . .

Interpreting forceful hand signals, players shouted the first words that came to their minds. In Mason City, Iowa, charades was the game of choice at the annual New Year's Eve Party. Fourteen couples rotated among homes for elegant festivities. Champagne flowed when the Times Square ball dropped, televised in snowy black and white. The food was as gourmet as could be had from the local Fareway, Piggly Wiggly, or mail-order from Neiman Marcus. The clothes were fancy too. Ladies wore sparkly cocktail dresses and gents stopped just short of tuxes.

Toward the end of the decade, community cookbooks cast a more sophisticated eye on food and entertainment. In recipes collected by members of symphony friends, resort associates and faculty wives, cocktails are mentioned—although they remained silent on details of their concoction. The nibbles "to be served with your best cocktails" were decidedly upscale.

Shrimp and Cucumber Spread

YIELD: ABOUT 1¼ CUPS

½ cup finely diced cucumbers
1 (5-ounce) can shrimp

½ cup mayonnaise
toasted bread or crackers

Peel and seed the cucumber before dicing. Cut in ⅛-inch dice; wrap in a sturdy paper towel and squeeze out the excess juice. Drain the shrimp and remove any shells or veins. Cut the shrimp into small pieces, the same size as the cucumber dice. Mix with mayonnaise and chill until ready to serve. Spread on hot buttered toast or crackers.

Parsley Cheese Strip Tassies

SERVES 10 TO 12 AS AN APPETIZER

2 tablespoons softened butter

⅔ cup grated sharp cheddar cheese

1 tablespoon cream

1 teaspoon prepared mustard

¼ teaspoon Worcestershire sauce or more to taste

½ teaspoon grated onion or more to taste

1 to 2 tablespoons minced fresh parsley

12 slices of thin, sturdy bread such as Pepperidge Farm thin-sliced white

Mix butter, cheese, cream, mustard, Worcestershire sauce, onion and parsley. Spread very thinly on bread slices and then cut each slice into four thin strips. Place strips on an ungreased baking sheet and put under the broiler until the cheese melts and turns just golden brown. These have a tendency to burn, so keep the broiler on low and have the baking sheet about 4 to 5 inches away.

Circle 3 of St. Andrews Guild will serve dinner Wednesday evening at the meeting of the Cloquet Chamber of Commerce. The menu will include Swiss steak, mashed potatoes, gravy, carrots, pineapple salad, pickles, fruit cocktail pudding and French bread. The program will be lifesaving awards to two Cloquet boys and a discussion of the proposed Scanlon-Cloquet consolidation.

CLOQUET (MINNESOTA) PINE KNOT, JUNE 28, 1955

Italian Olives

YIELD: ABOUT 2 QUART JARS FILLED
WITH OLIVES AND MARINADE

2 cups vinegar
⅜ cup olive oil
1 teaspoon salt
1 tablespoon minced parsley
1½ tablespoons dried oregano
½ teaspoon dried thyme
2½ tablespoons sugar
3 cloves garlic, mashed
36 ounces green and black olives, drained
celery ribs, sliced into ¼-inch thick crescents
green pepper slices, ¼-inch thick

Mix vinegar, oil, salt, parsley, oregano, thyme, sugar and garlic. Pour marinade over olives. Put in a covered jar, refrigerate and shake from time to time. Olives keep in refrigerator for up to two weeks. Bring to room temperature before serving. The day before using, add celery and green pepper.

Magic Blue Cheese Wafers

YIELD: **ABOUT 6 DOZEN WAFERS**

1 cup sifted flour
¼ cup cold butter
3 ounces chilled blue cheese
4 tablespoons cold milk, approximately
sesame seeds

Put flour into a medium mixing bowl. Cut butter and cheese into small pieces and add to flour. Using a wire pie-crust blender or two knives, cut butter and cheese into flour until mixture looks like cornmeal. Carefully add just enough milk to hold mixture together. Form dough into a 1¼-inch-diameter cylinder, wrap in foil or plastic wrap and freeze for several hours.

When ready to make wafers, preheat the oven to 400°F. Cut ⅛-inch-thick slices from the dough roll and place on an ungreased baking sheet. Sprinkle with sesame seeds, lightly pressing them into the unbaked dough. Bake for 5 to 6 minutes until wafers are just beginning to brown. Store wafers in an airtight container. Dough cylinders will keep in the freezer for several weeks.

Surprise Anniversary Potluck

Mr. and Mrs. John W. Ress of the Truman community received 30th wedding anniversary honors when friends planned a surprise party for them. The entertainment consisted of songs and recitations presented by various guests. Especially notable was Mrs. Lenore Lund's recitation "Beg Your Pardon" and Delores Long's singing of "Twenty-Four Hours of Sunshine." Mrs. Albert Ress and Mrs. William Reinke performed a skit "A Future Evening with the Resses." Joyce Herder provided the accordion music.

Noodle Ring with Creamed Chicken

SERVES 10 TO 12

NOTE: The noodle mixture also bakes up equally well in a rectangular pan to be served as squares, or in a 2-quart casserole where it could be turned upside down and cut into wedges. Serve this dish with a green salad or Jell-O mold, bread, Rhubarb Crunch for dessert and Roman Punch.

NOODLE RING:

1 pound noodles

3 eggs

¾ cup evaporated milk

¼ cup water

½ tablespoon Worcestershire sauce

dash of salt and pepper

2 tablespoons catsup

1 cup grated cheese—American, Swiss, mozzarella
 or even low-fat slices will work

Preheat oven to 350°F. Cook noodles as directed on the package and drain. While the noodles are cooking, mix other ingredients. Gently stir this sauce into the noodles and carefully pack mixture into a buttered 5- to 6-cup ring mold. Set the ring mold into a pan of hot water and place in the oven so that it will cook more evenly (see page 135 for tips). Bake until the noodles and sauce have formed a firm loaf, about 45 to 55 minutes. Remove from oven and run a sharp knife around the edge to loosen before carefully unmolding onto a serving plate. Fill the center with creamed chicken.

CREAMED CHICKEN:
4 cups cooked chicken (from 4- to 5-pound hen)
½ cup butter or chicken fat
4 tablespoons flour
2 egg yolks, lightly beaten
3 cups chicken stock or evaporated milk
3 tablespoons minced celery
3 tablespoons minced green pepper
¼ cup pimento, cut into thin strips (reserve a few strips for garnish)
1 (7-ounce) can mushrooms
1 tablespoon minced parsley
salt to taste
dash paprika
green pepper, finely cut

Cut cooked chicken in cubes. Melt butter in a large frying pan. Add flour and stir until blended. Mix the egg yolks with the chicken stock or milk, add to pan, and cook until thickened, stirring constantly. Fold in cubed chicken, celery, green pepper, pimento, mushrooms, parsley and salt. Pour into center of the noodle ring. Sprinkle tiny bits of pimento and paprika over chicken and finely cut green pepper over noodle ring.

Rhubarb Crunch

YIELD: 16 (2-INCH) SQUARES

1 cup white sugar

2 tablespoons cornstarch

1 cup water

1 teaspoon vanilla

1 cup sifted flour

¾ cup quick-cooking oats, not instant

1 cup brown sugar, firmly packed

1 teaspoon cinnamon

½ cup melted butter or shortening

4 cups rhubarb cut into ¼-inch dice

Preheat oven to 350°F. Grease an 8-inch square pan that is at least 3 inches deep (see page 113 for tips). Put white sugar and cornstarch into a 2-quart saucepan and whisk together. Gradually add water and cook over medium heat, stirring constantly, until this sauce is thickened. Remove from heat, cool slightly and add vanilla. Combine flour, oats, brown sugar and cinnamon in a small mixing bowl. Slowly pour melted butter over the dry ingredients, stirring with a fork until well blended and crumbly. Pour half the crumb mixture into the bottom of the pan and press firmly. Sprinkle diced rhubarb over the top. Next, pour on the cooled sugar sauce, then sprinkle the remaining crumb mixture on top. Bake for 55 to 60 minutes. Top will be brown and the rhubarb will bubble around the sides. Cool for at least 30 minutes before serving. Cut into squares and serve warm or cold with whipped cream or ice cream.

Roman Punch

YIELD: ABOUT 10 (½-CUP) SERVINGS

1 cup sugar

2 cups hot water

2 cups cold strong tea

1 cup orange juice

⅛ cup lemon juice

1 tablespoon rum extract

1 quart ginger ale

Combine the sugar and water in a 2-quart saucepan. Bring to a boil over medium heat. Cook for 5 minutes. Cool and add tea, orange juice, lemon juice and rum extract. This base can be refrigerated for up to three days. Just before serving add an equal part or more of ginger ale.

Teen Birthday Costume Party

Marilyn Olmer celebrated her fourteenth birthday at a Hawaiian-themed party. Eighteen guests arrived in Hawaiian costumes. Hula dolls served as placecards and guests received straw hats and leis as favors. During the lunch, Hawaiian records were played. The guests vied for prizes in games and various contests including best costume. Later they enjoyed listening and dancing to popular records.

The music tells it all. The 1950s was a decade of change. Top songs in 1950 included the Weavers' "Goodnight Irene," followed by Nat King Cole's "Mona Lisa." By 1955 Perez Prado topped the Billboard charts with "Cherry Pink and Apple Blossom White," but Bill Haley's "Rock around the Clock" was right behind. The next year Elvis held both the top spots with "Heartbreak Hotel" and "Don't Be Cruel." Moms who once made cookies for the kiddies now provided substantial treats for teenagers wearing bobby sox and dancing to 45s in basement rec rooms. Perhaps, now and again, the rock and roll was punctuated with the gentle clink of pop bottles spinning on the linoleum floor. The world would never be the same.

Green Dragon Chip Dip

YIELD: ABOUT 1 CUP

1 ripe avocado, mashed
1 (3-ounce) package cream cheese, softened
3 tablespoons mayonnaise
dash lemon juice or vinegar
¼ teaspoon seasoned salt such as Lawry's
½ teaspoon pepper

Combine all ingredients and blend until smooth. Put into serving bowl, cover with piece of plastic wrap pressed firmly down on the surface to prevent dip from turning dark and chill for 2 hours. Serve with potato chips for dipping.

7-Up Party Punch

YIELD: 12 (½-CUP) SERVINGS

1 pint lemon or orange sherbet
6 (8-ounce) bottles of 7-Up

Put sherbet in a large punch bowl. Pour the 7-Up over it and stir gently.

Teenage Special Burger Bake

SERVES 12

2 pounds lean hamburger
1 can cream-style corn
1 can tomato soup
1 small green pepper, diced
1 medium onion, diced

½ pound grated cheese
1 egg
1 teaspoon salt
8 ounces chow mein noodles

MUSHROOM SAUCE:
1 can cream of mushroom soup
½ cup cheese

Mix together hamburger, corn, soup, green pepper, onion, cheese, egg and salt. Put in ungreased 13x9-inch pan. Sprinkle chow mein noodles on top. Bake 1¼ to 1½ hours. Combine mushroom soup and cheese and heat until cheese is just melted. Cut Burger Bake into 12 pieces. Serve with hot Mushroom Sauce.

Ladies' Club Luncheons

The Mar-Kay study club met at the home of Mrs. James Stahl. After luncheon Mrs. Clement Nell presented the program on "Picasso and Other Abstract Artists." The afternoon closed with dessert and discussion.

Bridge or study group lunches were three-course events in midwestern small towns. Polished silver flatware, Haviland china and cloth napkins accompanied meals that took days of planning and hours of preparation. One participant took extreme exception when a guest called her precisely sauced lamb ragout "just a stew." No one would make that mistake with this curry.

Curried Lamb Luncheon Dish

SERVES 8 TO 10

2 pounds lamb shoulder cut into cubes

salt and pepper to taste

4 tablespoons vegetable oil

1 cup diced onion

2 cups diced celery

1½ cups water, divided

½ teaspoon curry powder

½ teaspoon oregano

1 bay leaf (remove before serving)

4 tablespoons flour

1 to 2 tablespoons Kitchen Bouquet

½ cup pickle relish, chutney or orange marmalade

4 cups cooked rice or noodles

Sprinkle the lamb with salt and pepper. Heat vegetable oil over medium heat in a large heavy frying pan with a lid. Brown the meat on all sides. Remove meat and add onion and celery. Cook until onion becomes translucent and tender. Turn heat to very low, return the lamb to the pan and add 1 cup of the water. Stir gently to blend. Cover, lower heat and simmer 1 hour. Mix seasonings and flour in a jar with a tight-fitting lid. Add ½ cup cold water and Kitchen Bouquet, a browning and seasoning sauce, for better color. Shake well until the flour is dissolved. Stir into lamb and cook until thickened. Stir in relish, chutney or orange marmalade. Serve over rice or noodles.

A pink and blue shower was given in honor of Mrs. William Kramer and Mrs. Al Larson. After the dessert luncheon the ladies played cards.

TRUMAN (MINNESOTA) INDEPENDENT, JANUARY 10, 1950

This is a lovely arranged salad. Amounts given are enough for eight servings—or two duplicate bridge tables. Shopping for fresh fruit was an adventure in the mid-sized towns of 1950s Iowa. My friend Nell recalled her quest to find the perfect fresh pineapple. The produce man at the Piggly Wiggly offered to cut the fruit in half to assure her that it was of good quality. She took him up on his offer. He bisected three pineapples, all of them rotten. She reluctantly changed her menu rather than continue to put him, and his fruit, to the test.

Fresh Fruit Salad

SERVES 8

1 (3-ounce) package Philadelphia cream cheese, softened
¼ cup finely chopped walnuts
1 pound dark sweet cherries
8 fresh apricots or peaches
8 large lettuce leaves
1 pineapple, peeled, cored, cut in rings and each ring cut in half
½ large cantaloupe cut into spears
1 pound green grapes
1 pint strawberries
½ large honeydew melon scooped into melon balls

Blend cream cheese and walnuts with a fork to make a filling for some of the fruit. Cut the cherries and apricots in half and remove the pits. Stuff them with the nut-and-cheese mixture. Place a large lettuce leaf on each plate and arrange the following on it: 2 or 3 pineapple half-rings, 1 or 2 cantaloupe spears, a dozen grapes, 3 or 4 strawberries, 4 melon balls, 6 stuffed cherry halves and 2 stuffed apricot halves. Dress with the Honey Salad Dressing or mayonnaise, if desired.

Honey Salad Dressing

YIELD: ABOUT 1 ½ CUPS

⅔ cup sugar

1 teaspoon dry mustard

1 teaspoon paprika

1 teaspoon celery seed

½ cup honey

5 tablespoons vinegar

1 teaspoon lemon juice

1 cup vegetable oil

Combine sugar, dry mustard, paprika and celery seed in a blender. Add honey, vinegar and lemon juice and pulse until just blended. With the blender running, slowly pour in the vegetable oil. Blend until the dressing is smooth. Unused portions keep in refrigerator for up to a week.

Pineapple-Cranberry Sipper

YIELD: 8 (½-CUP) SERVINGS

2 cups unsweetened pineapple juice

2 cups sweetened cranberry juice

¼ teaspoon whole cloves

1 teaspoon lemon juice

Combine all ingredients. Chill for at least one hour. When ready to serve, strain and serve over ice.

After spending hours and having fits over the salad and main courses, a clever hostess would have served this delicious cake that makes its own sauce.

Chocolate Sundae Pudding

SERVES 9

1 cup flour

2 teaspoons baking powder

¼ teaspoon salt

¾ cup white sugar

1 egg

½ cup milk

2 tablespoons melted butter or shortening

½ to 1 cup nutmeats

6 tablespoons cocoa

1 cup brown sugar, firmly packed

1¾ cup hot water

Preheat oven to 350°F. Grease a 9×9-inch pan before baking (see page 113 for tips). Sift flour, baking powder, salt and white sugar into a medium-size mixing bowl. Combine egg, milk and melted butter and stir into flour mixture. Add nutmeats and pour batter into pan. Combine cocoa and brown sugar and sprinkle over cake batter. Sprinkle the hot water evenly over cake batter by pouring it onto a tablespoon and allowing it to overflow onto the batter. Bake about 45 minutes until the cake is firm and the chocolate pudding is bubbly.

THE END OF AN ERA

Rae Katherine Eighmey

A GREAT MANY CHANGES TOOK PLACE in midwestern kitchens in the decade between the 1953 publication in English of Simone de Beauvoir's *The Second Sex* and the 1963 publication of Betty Friedan's *Feminine Mystique*. A soupçon of the concerns those writers expressed stirred in the mix of recipe, family and community goodwill. Candor began to creep into community cookbook narratives along with more sophisticated ingredients.

More than one cookbook editor included sentiments similar to the lines below from the 1958 University of Minnesota faculty wives cookbook.

As the 1950s drew to a close, the stage was set for more changes to come that would alter American business, politics and, most importantly, lives of women. In 1959 Jack Kilby of Texas Instruments and Robert Noyce of Fairchild Semiconductor applied for patents essential to the creation of the microchip—the heart of the personal computer. In January 1960, John Fitzgerald Kennedy challenged

A favorite topic of the faculty wife
(other than belles-lettres, children and human error)
is the preparation of good food.
Here we present her favorite recipes.
They have the patina of family laughter, gay parties,
and kitchen drudgery.
We hope you will prepare them, enjoy them
and pass them along, as we do now.

the heart of the nation as he announced his presidential bid. In June 1960 editor Judith Jones's heart beat a little faster when Julia Child's manuscript for *Mastering the Art of French Cooking* landed on her desk at Alfred Knopf.

In the heart of the country, midwestern women would respond to these changes and those to come. The tried and true recipes created and enjoyed in the 1950s took on new life when made by daughters and then granddaughters. Toted to potlucks in harvest gold and avocado green bowls, or in today's ubiquitous disposables, these classic dishes continue to bring us all back to the heart of the kitchen, where whatever comes to the potluck brings us to the paradise of fellowship and home.

Quiche Lorraine

SERVES 8

6 slices bacon

12 thin slices Swiss or Gruyere cheese

1 (9-inch) pie crust

4 eggs

1 tablespoon flour

½ teaspoon nutmeg

½ teaspoon salt

Cayenne pepper, a very few grains

2 cups light cream

1½ tablespoons butter, melted

Preheat oven to 375°F. Cook bacon until crisp and drain on paper towels. Slice cheese into pieces the same size as bacon strips. Cover pie crust with overlapping slices of bacon and cheese. Beat together eggs, flour, nutmeg, salt and cayenne. Add cream and melted butter. Pour this custard carefully over the cheese and bacon. Bake until custard is set and top is nicely browned, about 40 minutes. May be made ahead of time and refrigerated or frozen. At serving time, heat in slow oven and cut into 8 pieces. Serve warm.

Index to Recipes